Poland

Poland

BY MARTIN HINTZ

Enchantment of the World
Second Series

Children's Press®

A Division of Grolier Publishing

NEW YORK   LONDON   HONG KONG   SYDNEY
DANBURY, CONNECTICUT

To Mariusz, Tadeusz, Greta, Jozef, Icek, Froim,
Chaim, Helena, Jacek, Anna, and all the other children who
died in Poland during World War II.
The memory of their spirits remains bright.

Consultant: Alexander B. Murphy, Professor, Department of Geography, University of
Oregon, College of Arts and Sciences, Eugene, Oregon

Visit the Children's Press web site at http://publishing.grolier.com

Please note: *All statistics are as up-to-date as possible at the time of publication.*

Library of Congress Cataloging-in-Publication Data

Hintz, Martin.
      Poland/by Martin Hintz.
      p. cm. — (Enchantment of the world. Second series)
      Includes bibliographical references and index.
Summary: Describes the history, geography, economy, plants and animals, language,
      religion, sports, arts, and people of this central European country which
      has ties to both East and West.
      ISBN 0-516-20605-2
      1. Poland—Juvenile literature. [1. Poland.] I. Title. II. Series
      DK4147.H56 1998
      943.8—dc21   97-25559
                                                 CIP
                                               AC

Acknowledgments

The author wishes to thank the many persons who assisted in preparation of this manuscript. A special nod goes to Krystyna Gutt, who reviewed the initial manuscript and to all the friendly Poles who proudly showed off their country on the author's visits to their homeland. Thanks also to Dan Hintz for his assistance.

Contents

Cover photo:
Malbork Castle

Mountainous landscape in Poland

Polish girls enjoying a spring festival

Hello to Poland

Poland's history is a seesaw. Sometimes, everything seems wonderful. At other times, the most terrible things happen. Yet, the Polish people have remained proud and independent through out their up-and-down history.

THIS HAS NOT ALWAYS BEEN EASY. INVASIONS, OPPRESSION, and poverty never do anyone any good. Polish creativity, artistic accomplishments, and scientific endeavors reached great heights, however, whenever they were encouraged and allowed to flourish. Bravery and street smarts always got the Poles through the tough times. That made the good years even better. Unfortunately, the Poles occasionally brought difficulties on themselves.

Long ago, Polish nobles often fought among themselves. They did not want to give up any of their personal power for the common good of the country. This chaos allowed outsiders to move in and take over. Yet this infighting and greed for power were not limited to the wealthy. Ordinary Poles dreamed of independence and freedom while under an oppressor's thumb. Yet they often forgot their idealism when it came to developing a responsible government, even as opportunities presented themselves.

Even hundreds of years ago, Polish cities were cosmopolitan. Their business was business. Merchants and traders from all corners

The port at Gdansk

of the world rubbed shoulders in the markets, on the docks, and wherever else deals could be made. Caravans came from east and west; travelers moved from north to south. They passed through Kraków (Cracow), Wroclaw (Breslau), Warsaw, and the great Baltic Sea ports, bringing word of what was happening in the world to the cities. Most of Poland was rural at the time, however, and far removed from all this eye-opening activity.

Isolated Peasants

The countryside, with its vast open plains, high mountains, and thick forests, isolated Polish peasants for centuries. They became wary of outsiders, fearful of anything new. This was often for good reason. Outsiders often meant danger. This made them look inward for almost everything good. On one hand, this was beneficial. It created a self-help attitude and protected the peasants from harm. The family and home were more important than anything else.

But this isolation was negative, as well. Sometimes, villagers were suspicious of the people in towns just down the road or in hamlets over the next hill. It was easy

The Polish countryside is accented by beautiful mountains and fertile plains.

POLAND

FINLAND
Helsinki ★

LATVIA

Stockholm ★

SWEDEN

LITHUANIA

DENMARK

BELARUS

Copenhagen ★

Baltic Sea

Pomeranian Bay

Gulf of Gdansk

Gdynia ○
Gdansk ●

RUSSIA

Olsztyn ●   ○ L. Mamry

Walcz ○
Bydgoszcz ●
Szczecin ●

Lubawa ●   Masurian Lakes

Torun ●

Bialystok ●

Gniezno ●
Berlin ★
Warta   Poznan ●
Oder   Vistula

Bug

POLAND   Warsaw ★

GERMANY

Lodz ●

Radom ●

Wroclaw ●

Lublin ●

Suchedniow ○
Zagnansk ○

Opole ●   Gliwice ●
Katowice ●

Sandmierz ○

Zamosc ●

SUDETAN MTS.

CZECH. REP.

Kraków (Cracow) ●
Wadowice ○

UKRAINE

▲ Rysy Peak
CARPATHIAN MTS.

SLOVAKIA

POLAND

0 —————— 400 miles

0 —————— 600 kilometers

HUNGARY   ROMANIA

Geopolitical map
of Poland

to fall into an "us or them" attitude. Even within a single community, Christians might be wary of their Jewish neighbors. All this made thinking of a broader national ideal beyond the understanding of many Poles. This was true for generations who never had the opportunity to learn about the positive points of others.

Political and social turmoil has occurred during almost every other generation through Poland's thousand-year history. At one time or another, the Poles have been ruled either by kindly kings or despotic dictators. They amassed horizon-to-horizon territories, only to have large chunks of land gobbled up by stronger, greedy neighbors.

A Glorious Kingdom

Poland of the Middle Ages was one of the most glorious kingdoms in Europe. The Polish high court was dazzling for its energy and enthusiastic outlook on life. There seemed room for everyone, for great ideas, for magnificent opportunities. Talented artists painted. Scholars pondered great thoughts. And

brilliant musicians performed in opera halls and on concert stages. Within the thick castle walls, table-groaning banquets were ordinary occurrences. Living in Poland then, at least for the upper class, was like being on a cruise ship where everything seemed wonderful.

But this lifestyle was just as isolating and limiting for the rich and powerful as the deep valleys and thick woods were for the peasants. Outside the manor houses, ordinary Poles often lacked good shelter or food.

Malbork Castle

Poland's brief period of independence after World War I was enlightening, invigorating, and exciting. It seemed that finally Poland was on the road toward a bright future. The backwardness of rural life was on its slow, heavy way to being pried open. Everything seemed possible.

Then came the Nazi occupation of Poland during the bloody days of World War II. Millions of Poles died on the battlefields and in the concentration camps.

That terror was followed by heavy-fisted Communist rule, imposed from the outside—again. For forty years, it was impossible for the ordinary Poles to have a say in the way things were done in their country. To be bravely outspoken in the face of this oppression meant prison, or worse. It was not until the 1990s, after a long political and emotional struggle, that Poles were again able to assert themselves as a truly free people. They are still struggling to find themselves a national niche in a fast-paced, modern world.

A Future with Many Questions

What will happen to Poland, now that the way is clear for economic, social, and political freedom? Will the mistakes of the past be repeated? Will the Poles fight among themselves again? Will outsiders ever again be able to dictate what happens in this country? The Polish people themselves have to determine where they are going. It will be a long, hard process, but Poles are used to such challenges.

Modern Poland is blessed with significant natural resources and highly educated citizens who are now ready to look outward. The country's long-standing tradition of being a "crossroads country," one influenced by many cultures, has always been a powerful attribute. This combination contributes to making Poland a special place.

Poland's time-honored ethic that working hard brings rewards has benefited the rest of the world. Through the years, hundreds of thousands of Poles emigrated to Canada, the United States, Australia, and other countries. They carried the best of their homeland with them and carved out new lives for themselves. Subsequently, elements of Polish heritage can be found almost everywhere, from foods to crafts, from dances to artwork, from literary classics to scientific discoveries. The Poles eagerly share what they have. Many other nations are the better for this spirit, brought by their eager, new citizens.

No matter what happened in the past, the image of a brave Poland was a beacon to freedom lovers everywhere. Today, that traditional courage in the face of adversity remains an example for everyone.

A Polish neighborhood in Toronto, Canada

Poland as a Nation

On a map, Poland is a tight square. But within this boxy shape are forested mountains, blue lakes, sandy plains, flower-filled highland meadows, and rich farmland. This geographic patchwork is a quilt sewn together by the snakelike Barycz, Gwda, Zonzo, Stupa, òyna, and other picturesque streams and rivers.

POLAND IS A CROSSROADS COUNTRY, LYING ON THE GREAT European Plain. In Polish, the name of the country means "land of fields." Located in central Europe, Poland is tied both to the West and the East. It is the seventh-largest nation on the continent. Its boundaries have changed many times through the centuries because of wars and occupation by outsiders. Poland sprawls over 120,728 square miles (312,684 sq km). Today, the country is twice the size of England. It is about as large as the state of New Mexico.

Many vacationers enjoy the Baltic coast.

Poland's Borders

The deep gray waters of the Baltic Sea and a portion of the Lithuanian border make up Poland's northern border. The 310-mile (500-km) long Baltic seacoast stretches from the Gulf of Gdansk in the east to the Gulf of Pomorze (Pomerania) in the west. This rugged coastline is a favorite landscape subject for painters and photographers. Vacationers from around Europe flock to the sandy

beaches there to spread their blankets and sunbathe. Thick pine forests creep almost to the water's edge in some places, giving much of the northern region a wild appearance. Brackish, or salty, lagoons speckle the area making the surrounding land unfit for farming. Yet the Baltic area has also long been the traditional industrial center of Poland. There is easy access to seaports and to the country's rich natural resources, including coal and timber.

Poland's eastern border touches the countries of Belarus and Ukraine, once republics of the former Soviet Union. Poland's western border is shared with Germany.

Geographical Features

Total Area: 120,728 square miles (312,684 sq km)

Population Density: 312 person per square mile (120 per sq km)

Highest Elevation: Rysy Peak, 8,196 feet (2,499 m)

Lowest Point: Vistula Delta, 6 feet (1.8 m)

Longest River: Vistula, 665 miles (1,070 km)

Largest Lake: Lake Sniardwy, 41 square miles (16 sq km)

Largest City: Warsaw, 2,316,000 (1995)

Average Temperatures:
Winter: 23° to 30° F (−5° to −1°C)
Summer: 63° to 68° F (17° to 20° C)

Average Annual Precipitation: 24 inches (610 mm)

Area with Highest Annual Precipitation:
Carpathian Mountains, 47 to 59 inches (1,195 to 1,500 mm)

Along both frontiers, flat fields and grassy plains stretch from horizon to horizon. This lack of any natural topographical defense has allowed Poland's warlike neighbors to invade the country easily. Ancient tribes, such as the Tatars, and more modern enemies, have occupied chunks of Poland. Nothing but the bravery of the Poles stopped calvary or tanks, once the armies attacked.

The southern border, however, is more rugged and difficult to cross. The Sudeten and Carpathian

The Tatra Mountains

mountains mark the dividing line with the Czech Republic and Slovakia. The Carpathians, which date back millions of years, are an extension of the Alps. Mount Sniezka, one of Poland's tallest peaks, is here. The mountain rises 5,259 feet (1,603 m). To the west of the Carpathians are the Sudeten Mountains. The granite ridges of Poland's steep eastern mountains are called the High Tatras. Rysy Peak, at 8,196 feet (2,499 m), is found in this mountain chain. This is Poland's highest mountain. The West and East Beskids are other mountain ranges found in the eastern regions of Poland. These mountains are blanketed with snow throughout the winter. The snow does not start melting until May. In the high mountains are doliny, which are open, flat valleys tucked between the towering ridges. Rimmed by pine trees, they create an island of quiet where a hiker can spot eagles and other wildlife.

The Mighty Vistula

In eastern Poland, the Vistula (Wisla) River flows out of the soaring Carpathian Mountains. It flows for about 665 miles (1070 km), emptying into the Gulf of Gdańsk (Danzig) after traversing a wide area made of marshland dotted with tiny islands. This part of the Vistula River is known as the Dead Martwa Wisla, where only small, flat-bottom boats can travel. Rare golden amber, the fossilized resin from ancient pine trees, can be found near a lagoon just before the water enters into the gulf. Amber is used in jewelry.

A spiderweb of tributaries, or smaller rivers, feed into the mighty Vistula, which divides the country in half. The Vistula is the country's longest river, running from its headwaters in the Carpathian Mountains to the Baltic Sea. Among the country's other major waterways are the Dunajec, San, Wieprz, Pilica, and Bug rivers. The Oder (Odra) River flows through western Poland. Its tributaries include the two branches of the rolling Neisse (Nysa) River, plus the Bóber, Warta, and Noté rivers.

Lakes in Poland

Sparkling lakes dot the Polish landscape with their bright reflective surfaces. More than seven thousand were formed by glaciers that crawled across the land thousands of years ago. During those days of the great ice ages, towering sheets of ice dug out shallow depressions. They then filled with melting snow and rainwater. There are numerous marshes and bogs, rimmed by thick reeds and rushes. On the northeast border of the country are the Masurian Lakes, the largest of which is the 47-mile (75.2-km) wide Lake Sniardwy. Mamry is another large lake in the region, one favored by fishing fans for its carp and trout. More than half of the other lakes are found in the

Many forests in Poland have been hurt by pollution and acid rain.

western Pomeranian and Wielkopolska-Kujawski lake districts.

The other large bodies of shallow waterways form the Leczycko-Kujawski lake district located near the ancient market town of Lublin, adjacent to the Belarus border. Dense forests run to the lakeshores. Tourists flock to these areas for water sports, fishing, and hunting. Poles enjoy the natural beauty of the lakes and their surroundings. The Lublin Plateau is a major part of Poland's geography, rising from 650 to 1,600 feet (200 to 500 m) above the flatlands around Lublin.

Environmental Concerns

Poles are quite concerned about their environment. They know it will take millions of dollars to repair the damage done over generations of war and industrial abuse. Severe air and water pollution have damaged thousands of acres. The Black Triangle is a broad plateau adjoining Germany and the Czech Republic. Coal-fired power plants here poured sulfur dioxide into the atmosphere, which destroyed forestland with the resulting acid rain. It is estimated that more than half of Poland's fir trees have lost a quarter of their needles because of air pollution. If the trees die, soil erosion is sure to follow.

Automobiles also contribute to the problem. There are at least 5 million private cars in Poland. Many are not mechanically serviced well, so dirty emissions have also caused air pollution.

Today, however, the Polish government actively tries to protect the purity of water and air cleanliness. Environmental laws are strictly enforced. Polluters are legally required to clean up any mess they make. Companies have to report how any expansion or construction will affect the surroundings. If there is a problem, changes have to be made immediately.

Poland is now a major market for pollution-control equipment made in other countries. Poles buy screens, filters, and other devices to be installed in Polish factories. This helps keep the undamaged landscape fresh and safe and returns damaged land and water back to a purer state. Poland has

Farming is still a major industry in Poland.

joined other countries in working toward environmental cleanliness. The country participates in many treaties covering the ocean, hazardous wastes, nuclear test bans, and wetlands.

Farming Land

More than 50 percent of the land can be farmed. About 24 percent is covered with hardwood and evergreen forests. The Bledowska Desert, the only place in central Europe with

Kraków, Poznan, and Wroclaw

Kraków *(right)* is the third largest city in Poland. According to a legend, a terrible monster lived under the walls of Wawel, an ancient castle overlooking the Vistula River. A dashing young Polish prince named Krak killed the monster after a fierce fight. Because of his bravery, the town around the castle was named after him, and he became king. Today, the city is known as Kraków. Thousands of years ago, Stone Age people lived where the city was eventually founded in the eighth century.

From its start as just a cluster of huts, Kraków eventually became the capital of Poland for a time. It remained the seat of kings until 1596. It is noted for its architecture, museums, churches, and monasteries. The city's first cathedral was built in 1056. The city's spectacular marketplace is in the center of Old Town *(above left and right)*, with the Cloth Hall being the primary building. Today, it houses souvenir shops on the first floor. The building also contains a gallery of Polish paintings dating from the eighteenth and nineteenth centuries. The city's Jagiellonian University is one of the oldest learning centers in Europe, attended by

50,000 students. The university was founded in 1364 by King Casimir the Great.

The average daily January temperature in Kraków is 20°F (−7°C) and 60°F (16°C) in June. It is 778 feet (1245 m) above sea level.

The history of Poznan reaches back 1,000 years and the city was the residence of the Polish kings for a time. The city of 589,700 is a center of commerce, learning, and culture. There are eight higher level schools as well as several research institutes, plus six major theaters and ten museums. The Poznan Philharmonic Orchestra and the city's Men and Boys Chorus are known throughout Europe. Poznan is also famous for its national and international trade fairs and its twenty sports stadiums and playing grounds.

The average daily temperature in January is 25°F (−4°C) and 60°F (16°C) in June. The city is 282 feet (451 m) above sea level.

Wroclaw is a beautiful city located in southwestern Poland on the Oder River in the Silesian Valley. There are a total of eighty-four bridges in Wroclaw. In Europe, only Italy's Venice and Russia's St. Petersburg have more bridges. The history of the city dates back to the year 1000. There are many historically significant homes in Wroclaw, including two small houses in which the Hansel and Gretel of folk legend supposedly once lived. Despite its age, the population of 643,600 seems young because about half the residents are under thirty years old. Wroclaw is filled with students attending one of the ten academies in the city. There are many museums, a philharmonic hall, an opera, an operetta and many theaters.

Average temperature in January is 22°F (−6°C) and 63°F (17°C) in June. Wroclaw is 394 feet (630 m) above sea level.

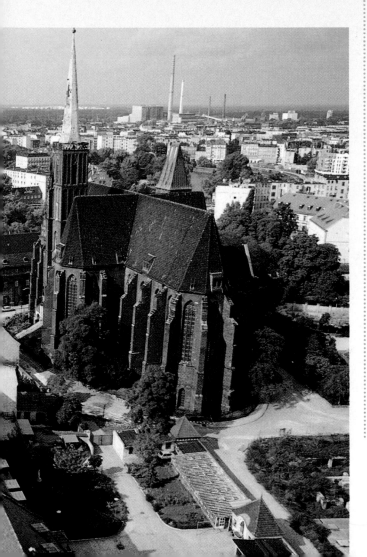

shifting sand dunes, covers 12.4 square miles (32 sq km). Travelers crossing this desert sometimes can see mirages called *fata morgana*. A mirage is an optical illusion caused by the reflection of light through layers of different air temperatures. In this rare Polish desert, an object might seem to be very close when it is actually far away.

Polish Climate

Poland's climate is similar to that of the middle of North America and the rest of Europe. The four major seasons are easy to tell apart. The summery months of June through August are typically warm and sometimes hot. The average temperature is between 60°F (16°C) and 70°F (21°C). Autumn runs from September through November and is usually sunny and dry with pleasant days and cool nights. Winter runs from December through March, with an average chilly temperature of 30°F (0°C). Deep snow is common across the country. Drifts do not melt in the mountains until the middle of April. In April and May, spring days are warm and sunny. But the nights during these months tend to be cool. The average rainfall in Poland ranges from 21 to 26 inches (53 to 66 cm) per year. Most of this rainfall occurs in the summer months.

Poland is capitalizing on its geographic position in northern Europe. It is growing economically stronger, with expanding trading connections in both the East and the West. This continues a tradition of being ready to accept possibilities and challenges. As such, Poland moves into the twenty-first century with optimism, based on a thousand-year history of capitalizing on what the country's natural richness has to offer. Sometimes, these gifts were not used wisely. But as the new Poland matures, its people see the need to nurture and protect all the wonders its geography contains.

Snow covers much of Poland during the winter months.

A Country of Green

Almost a quarter of Poland is carpeted with pine and hardwood trees. Thick stands of spruce, larch, and fir blanket the northeast along the Belarus-Polish frontier. Oak, beech, ash, elm, and maple trees dominate in the southern lowlands.

A shepherd tending to his sheep

THE RIVER VALLEYS, CARVED out by centuries of mud-brown waters, are shaded by the wide sweeping arms of weeping willows. Sweetly scented apple and other fruit orchards are scattered throughout the country. After the snow has melted in the mountains, a profusion of wildflowers grow on the rugged slopes. Ferns, brush, and brambles blossom once the weather turns mild. Sheep and cattle graze on the lush, green wild grasses found in the mountain pastures during the summer. The animals are brought to the valleys in the winter when deep snow piles up in the mountains.

A park containing about nine hundred oaks graces the town of Rogaun, 12 miles (20 km) south of Poznan. Each tree is very old. The gnarled trunks look their graceful age. Massive branches extend far out in all directions. The largest, most venerable tree measures 27 feet (8.3 m) around its base. Near it are two others almost as large. These three trees are about eight hundred years old. According to folklore, the trees sup-

posedly represent Lech, Czech, and Rus—the three brothers who laid the foundations for Poland, the Czech Republic, and Russia. Many Poles like to think of their country being like these ancient oaks. Both country and trees are strong, proud, and continue to grow every year.

Opposite: **An ancient oak tree in Rogaun**

Snowcapped Peaks

The wind-swept cliffs of the southern mountains are so high that little vegetation grows there beyond the tree line. Some of the peaks are snowcapped almost all year. But edelweiss peers out from cracks in the rock, dazzling the heavy gray-black background with its lively color. This small rugged mountain plant with white leaves is arranged in a star-shaped pattern around a tiny yellow center.

Edelweiss is a rugged but elegant mountain flower.

Picking mushrooms is a popular pastime.

Mushrooms

The woods surrounding Poland's many lakes are perfect for mushroom hunters. Everyone has a favorite spot, whether in the Piska Forest or the Tochola Woods. The town of Walcz is noted for its mushrooms, and serious mushroom pickers gather here annually. The edible mushrooms can be added to many recipes. A variety of little yellow mushrooms, the kurki, are stewed in fresh cream. At the beginning of July, the large, delicious borowiki appear. These highly prized mushrooms have a white stem and a brown cap called the pileus. They are dried at home or in the ovens of the local

The opienki mushroom

baker, to be added to some dish later on. The borowiki are soon followed by the red-capped kozlarz. An August mushroom, the maslak, is made into pickles. Picking continues until autumn's first ground frost puts even the rugged opienki into hibernation until the following year.

The Potato in Poland

Some plants are not native to Poland but were brought here centuries ago. King Jan Sobieski is credited with introducing the potato to Poland. After defeating the Turks at the Battle of Vienna in 1683, he returned home with more than a victory. He carried a bag of potato seedlings that he was given in tribute. The king planted the first crop at Wilanów, his royal estate near Warsaw. The vegetable did not gain much acceptance, however, until one hundred years later. It took Poland's last king, Stanislaw August Poniatowski, to encourage peas-

The potato is one of many crops in Poland.

A hippo at the Wroclaw Zoo

ants to grow potatoes on a widespread basis. Today, they are a major crop and part of every meal.

There are few animals living in their natural habitat in Poland because so much of the land is cultivated or inhabited. The country's largest zoos are in Warsaw, Lodz, Wroclaw, and Poznan. The birth of an animal is always special. The Wroclaw Zoo has a unique maternity clinic where bison, brown bears, giraffes, hippopotamuses, and camels have been born.

Wilder beasts live as far from humans as possible. A few rare wolves, bears, and wildcats are still found in the wilds of the Carpathian Mountains.

Marmot Mountains

The soaring peaks of the High Tatras are home to marmots. These small, fuzzy rodents look like a North American woodchuck or groundhog. The chipper, cheeky marmots peek out from the burrows amid the rocks and chatter with their neighbors.

Marmots live in the Tatra Mountains.

Chamois also live in the High Tatras, leaping from ledge to ledge across the narrow cliffs. The chamois are small antelopes that seldom grow more than 2 feet (0.6 m) high. Their horns stick straight up, with a backward bend at the tip. Fearless, wild sheep also live in the craigs and mountain valleys.

The chamois are also native to the Tatras.

Over the centuries, hunters almost wiped out these wild animals, pushing them deeper and deeper into the recesses of the country. But in 1889, the land around the resort town of Zakopane was purchased by Count Wladyslaw Zamoyski. After his death, the count gave his land to the Polish nation for use as an animal preserve. The site was expanded in 1937. After World War II, the Tatra National Park was officially established on the site. It now covers 55,000 acres (22,258 ha) and is one

Tatra National Park

of the largest of the country's 12 national parks and 450 nature preserves. Hikers are cautioned to stay on the marked trails through the park so that they do not disturb the wildlife and plants.

An ancient ox-like animal called the auroch (AR-awk) and ponderous, giant bison used to roam over most of southern Poland. These beasts have long been extinct. A herd of about two hundred smaller European bison, however, still live in the thick oak woods of the Bialowieza Forest. The animals look remarkably like North American buffalo. They muscle through their forest enclosures on the way to the best patches of grazing land. The forest was once a royal hunting preserve where only Polish royalty could shoot the cumbersome creatures. Yet war knows no such restrictions. Starving soldiers in World War I killed and ate the entire herd. So, in 1929, three pairs of bison were purchased by the Polish government from other European zoos. The bison were then returned to the forest. After years of careful breeding, the Poles now have enough animals to share with forest preserves and zoos around the world.

Bison in the Bialowieza Forest

The elk is common in the forests of Poland.

Other Wildlife

The Kampinos Forest in southern Poland is a picturesque mixture of marshes, forests, and lakes. A few boar still rummage through the underbrush. With their sharp tusks and short tempers, boars can be very dangerous. But they are rare and hard to find. If one is spotted, it is wise to get out of the way… fast!

**The Chopin Monument
in Warsaw**

National Bird

The national bird of Poland is the eagle. It represents the royal founding of the country. According to folklore, Lech, leader of one of the three bands of ancient Slavs, once saw an eagle in a tree, which convinced him to stop in that place and make his home there. The site become Poland.

More numerous are the elk and deer, seen leaping over the brush whenever hikers startle them. Because of its thick, tangled undergrowth, the forest was nicknamed the Kampinos Jungle by Polish freedom fighters. Bands of partisans hid there during World War II, venturing out to harass the Nazi troops.

Parks and preserves provide delightful, eye-soothing dots of greenery in or near every village and town in Poland. Swans paddle about lazily in the heart of Lubawa in Poland's Pomerania district. Excursion boats chug past the extensive floral gardens outside Torun's Church of St. John. A small train runs under towering trees in the Swietokrzyskie (Holy Cross) Forest in the Kielce Mountains. Its old steam engine pulls several coaches along the 31-mile (50-km) ride from Zagnansk to Suchedniow. Lazienki Park in Warsaw was created between 1764 and 1795 under the watchful eye of King Stanislaus Augustus. The king loved flowers and wanted to be sure his subjects had the chance to enjoy them. The park's walkways meander past duck ponds and small stages for evening concerts.

Horses have played an important role in Poland's history. Hussars and uhlans were the country's cavalry, renowned for their bravery. Armed only with lances and swords, they even charged attacking German tanks during the early days of World War II. As the pages of the Polish story are turned, the horse is always there.

There are more than two million horses in Poland, the largest number in any European country. The main breed is the massive Wielkopolska, noted for its jumping abilities. Another is the Maloposka, which traces its bloodlines from Oriental, Hungarian, Austrian, and Arab horses.

Arabian horses are among the breeds raised on Polish stud farms.

Polish Stud Farms

Horses are raised on sprawling stud farms, where there are hundreds of acres of lush, green grass for feed. Many of these farms are in eastern Poland, where the herds can gallop across the wide, open spaces. Janow Podlaski is one of the largest and best-known stud farms, famous for its magnificent, perfectly proportioned stallions and mares. Every September, the stable holds an auction for horse lovers coming from around the world to bid on the stock. Some horses sell for a million dollars.

Once horses were the preserve of the rich, the only Poles able to afford to keep the animals. Now, there are numerous riding stables in Poland and many middle-class Poles ride for the sheer enjoyment of the sport. They enjoy racing, hunting, and leisurely rides through parks. The riders usually use the English-style saddles rather than the cowboy style of the western United States and Canada. Poland's Olympic contenders are always considered among the world's top horsemen and -women.

Stork nests can be spotted atop cottages throughout Poland. The giant, skinny-legged birds build their nests close to the house chimneys where they can be warm. The storks return to the same nests every year. Folklore says that when a stork comes back to a house, a baby will be born to the family who lives inside. This might be the origin of the tale that claims storks deliver babies.

Poles are proud that their country has such a rich natural heritage. However, there has been tension between developers and environmentalists under both the Communist and capitalist systems. Silesia has especially been affected by factories that spew pollution into the air. Poles know it is necessary to reconcile the importance of industrial growth and the value of preservation. Most are working hard to do that, but much remains to be done.

Opposite: **A stork nesting in a chimney**

The Ancient Land

One thousand years ago, Ibrahim Ibn-Jakub was a merchant and explorer with a yen for adventure. He traveled all over Europe looking for markets for his spices and silks from the Middle East. Ibn-Jakub visited Poland, pausing in his travel along the low banks of the dark-brown Vistula River. In his descriptive journal, Ibn-Jakub wrote, "This is a beautiful, strange country."

BUT EVEN IBN-JAKUB COULD BE CONSIDERED A LATECOMER to Poland. The country's history goes back much farther. Archaeologists have found Stone Age artifacts and Iron Age villages, which had been buried for centuries in bogs and marshes. When a marsh was drained in recent times, the scientists found household items, human and animal remains, and remnants of buildings. One entire town along the Dnieper River, Biskupin, was carefully rebuilt as a tourist and historical attraction, complete with a stockade and log houses. Coming here is like traveling in a time machine. By carefully looking around at the huts, a visitor can imagine what life was like those years long ago.

Restored ancient dwellings at Biskupin

A group of people called the Slavs (Slavonians) eventually settled much of northern and eastern Europe. One of their tribes was the Polanie, who were the ancestors of today's Poles. As the Polanie became stronger, they fought among themselves for power and land. Gradually, the Piast family gained the upper hand in these petty wars. Their banner flew over thousands of acres of rivers, lakes, farmland, and forest. This was the start of Poland as a nation.

The great-great-grandson of that first mighty Piast prince was Mieszko I. He converted to Christianity in A.D. 966 and gave greater freedom to Christian missionaries to work with his pagan subjects. Mieszko knew that the protection of the Roman Catholic Church was important, especially when facing enemies who were beginning to covet his lands. The next-door Germans were already strong enough to demand bribes or tributes, the payment of money in return for leaving Poland alone. Mieszko had no choice but to pay the tribute when confronted by his stronger neighbor.

Mieszko died in 992 and his son, Boleslaw the Brave, became Poland's ruler. He extended his reach and brought much-needed order to the rough, wild fringes of his territory. Under Boleslaw's reign, Poland finally became an independent nation. But that situation did not last long. Boleslaw's successors were weak and quarrelsome. They fought among themselves and again broke Poland into many smaller divisions. This made it easy for invaders to snatch off portions of land, much like wild dogs attacking a flock of frightened sheep.

Timeline of Important Dates in Polish History

2000 B.C.–1000 B.C. First Slavonic settlement is established in Poland.

6th century B.C. First fortified settlement is made (The Biskupin Fortress).

A.D. 963 Poland's first historic ruler, Mieszko I of the Piast dynasty, is crowned.

966 Lesser Poland converts to Christianity.

1013 First of the Russian-Polish wars begin.

1241 Mongols invade Poland.

1333 (March 3) Casimir the Great is crowned.

1364 Jagiellonion University, one of the oldest in Europe, is founded.

1374 Jagiellonians replace the Piasts on the royal throne of Poland.

1518 Reformation reaches Poland and rebellions spread throughout Poland.

1569 Poland and Lithuania unite.

1572 The Jagiellonion Dynasty ends and the elected monarchy begins.

1655 Sweden invades Poland.

1791 (May 3) The Seym, the Polish Parliament, adopt a constitution modeled after the U.S constitution, the second of its kind in the world.

1793– 1795 The new Polish Constitution is crushed by the partition of Poland by Russia, Prussia, and Austria.

1882 The first Polish revolutionary worker's party, Proletariat, is founded.

1918 (November 11) Poland is declared an independent republic.

1939 Poland is crushed in a lightning-quick attack by Nazi Germany and Russia, who then partition the country into two parts.

1941– 1944 The systematic murder of Jews begins in the concentration camps of Poland, killing almost 4 million people by 1944.

1944 (July) Poland is liberated from Nazi Germany and comes under indirect rule by the Soviet Union.

1945 (Jan 1) The Soviet sponsored Polish Committee of National Liberation takes over the government.

1980 (July) Solidarity, a trade union organization led by Lech Walesa is created.

1983 (October) Walesa is given Nobel Peace Prize.

1989 (August 24) The end of almost forty-five years of Communist domination comes with an election of the coalition government consisting of Solidarity, The United Peasants Party, and the Democratic Party.

1991 Poland's membership in the Warsaw Pact ends.

1994 Final withdrawal of Soviet troops is completed.

1995 (November 11) Lech Walesa loses presidency to Aleksander Kwasniewski, a former communist party member.

The seal of King Casimir the Great. It features the eagle, Poland's national bird.

From 1333 to 1370, Casimir the Great sat on the Polish throne. He was the last Piast king of Poland. He was strong enough to unite all the warring divisions of the country. It was said that "he found a Poland made of wood, but left behind one of stone." His reign was noted for its tolerance of many cultures, including that of the Jews. Subsequently, Poland became a center of Jewish culture. Unfortunately, Casimir died without any sons to take over the crown of Poland. So it was agreed by the other Polish nobles that Casimir's nephew, Louis of Hungary, would be king. Yet Louis also died without any heirs, except for his daughter, Jadwiga. She was just eleven years old when crowned ruler of Poland. Although she loved another man, Jadwiga was forced to marry a Lithuanian prince named Jagiello when she was fourteen. This made a strong alliance between their two countries.

Jadwiga was only eleven years old when she was crowned ruler of Poland.

Nicolaus Copernicus—The Father of Astronomy

Nicolaus Copernicus (Mikolaj Kopernik) was a Polish astronomer who lived from 1473 to 1543. His work supported the theory that the earth was round and that it revolved on an axis, an imaginary line through its middle. This theory went against many of the beliefs of his day, one of which stated the sun revolved around the earth, which stood still. He used geometry and trigonometry to prove his theories. This use of mathematics eventually became the fundamental concept of understanding how the universe functioned. Worried about opposition from the Church and the government, Copernicus kept his story a secret until he was an old man and had many years to perfect his serious studies. For his valuable insights, he is known as the Father of Astronomy.

Knights Defeated

Jagiello was a great general. He led the combined armies of Poland and Lithuania against the Teutonic Knights and other invaders. He defeated the Knights, a Germanic order of warriors, at Grunwald in 1410, considered one of the greatest battles of Polish history. The victory launched the two-hundred-year Jagiellenian dynasty. Poland's frontier burst at the seams as new territories were absorbed. The country was the largest in fifteenth century Europe. The treasury overflowed. The arts flourished. It was Poland's Golden Age.

Poland and Lithuania, 1410

Rulers of Poland

House of Piasts

Miesko I	962–992
Boleslav I	992–1025
Boleslav II	1058–1079
Boleslav III	1106–1138

Feudal Division of Poland	1138–1306
Vladislav I	1306–1333
Casimir the Great	1333–1370

House of Anjou

Louis I	1370–1382
also Louis I of Hungary	
Jadwiga	1384–1399

House of Jagiellonians

Vladislav II	1386–1434
Vladislav III	1434–1444
also King of Hungary	
Casimir IV	1446–1492

Sigismund I	1506–1548
Sigismund II	1548–1572

Elected Kings

Stephen Batory	1576–1586
Sigismund III Vasa	1587–1632
	1592–1598
	King of Sweden
Vladislav II Vasa	1632–1648
John II Casimir Vasa	1648–1668
John III Sobieski	1674–1696
Stanislav II	1764–1795
	Last king of Poland

Poland under Foreign Rule

Poland partitioned between Austria, Russia, and Prussia	1795
Grand Duchy of Warsaw created by Napoleon I	1807–1815
Declared part of Russian Empire	1815

Second Republic

Head of State Jozef Pilsudski	1918–1922
President Gabriel Narutowicz	1922
Stanislav Wojciechowski	1922–1926
Ignacy Moscicki	1926–1939
	dictator

Nazi Germany and Soviet Union invade Poland and partition the country	1939
Nazi Germany controls all of Poland	1941
Soviet Sponsored Polish Committee of National Liberation	January 1, 1945
Lech Walesa and Solidarity Party end 45 year rule of Communists	November 5, 1989

A scene from the Battle of Vienna

But Poland's luck did not last forever. Tatar horsemen thundered out of the east, torching Polish villages and killing every living thing in their path. Ottoman Turks roared up from the south, only to be narrowly defeated by the Poles at the bloody Battle of Vienna in 1683. This constant warfare and ongoing feuds between Poland's nobles pushed Poland into a political decline. Just as the country was being drained of its soldiers and money, Russia, Prussia, and Austria carved out huge chunks of Polish territory for themselves. So, by 1800, Poland as a country was gutted and no longer in existence.

Rebellious Poles allied themselves with Napoleon Bonaparte, the new ruler of France. With the aid of these Polish soldiers, Napoleon defeated the Prussians and Austrians in several important battles. He forced them to return some Polish lands. But Napoleon eventually met his match when he invaded Russia in 1812. Retreating with his army in ruins, Napoleon was unable to protect Poland. As a result, Poland was at the mercy of hungry outsiders. The Russians marched in, exercising total authority over the country. Uprisings sputtered and failed in 1830 and 1863. The people, however, remained fiercely proud of their heritage, their customs, their language, and their Catholic faith despite the oppression.

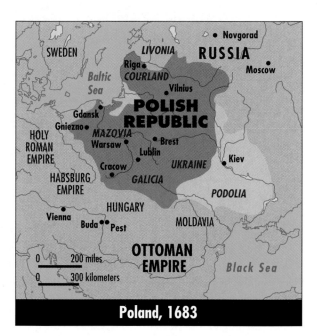

Poland, 1683

The Russian invasion of Poland

The Ancient Land **49**

Famous Poles

The United States and Canada have long had close relations with Poland. Thousands of Poles emigrated to both countries over the past 200 years. In the American Revolution, Polish military commanders such as Tadeusz Kosciuszko *(above left)* and Casimir Pulaski *(left)* fought for the American colonies. Pulaski was killed in a cavalry charge in the Battle of Savannah in 1779. Kosciuszko went back to his native country to lead several revolutions against the Austrians and Russians. He died in 1817 and is buried in Kraków's cathedral.

Scientist Marie Curie (Maria Sklodowska), was another famous Pole who lived much of her life away from her homeland. She and her French husband, Pierre Curie, studied radiation found in uranium ore. For their work, the couple *(above right)* won a Nobel Prize for science in 1903. After her husband died, Madame Curie continued her work. She became the first woman to become a teaching master at the famous Sorbonne University in Paris. In 1911, she won another Nobel Prize, this time in chemisty. Her work led to the development of X rays.

A Hero Appears

As it often happens when a national spirit seems doomed, a hero appears. Jozef Pilsudski was a great revolutionary leader in the early 1900s. During World War I, he led the Polish Legion of the Austrian army against the Russians. The Russians were eventually driven out the Polish homeland. However, the Germans and Austrians replaced them. Pilsudski refused to swear allegiance to the German emperor and was imprisoned. The war finally ground to a bloody halt, when Germany and her allies were defeated.

Famed Polish pianist Ignacy Jan Paderewski persuaded U. S. President Woodrow Wilson to take up the cause of Polish freedom after the war. With Wilson's encouragement, a Polish republic was formed. The old hero Pilsudski became the head of the new government. Pilsudski tried to retire in 1923, but he saw his country faced with more danger. Many problems worried him, so he took control of the Polish army and instituted a military government.

Jozel Pilsudski was a hero in World War I.

Ignacy Jan Paderewski

Poland 1921–1997

- ⧅ Poland, 1921–38
- ▢ Poland, 1997
- —— Borders, 1938
- ---- Borders of new states
- MOLDAVIA Names of new states

In its first eight years as a modern nation, Poland had thirteen governments. And there was even more trouble. Communists had staged a successful revolution in the old Russia, creating the Soviet Union. They then launched a short war against Poland but were defeated. The Nazi party took over Germany, wanting to reclaim lands lost during World War II. So Pilsudski returned to power, firmly ruling Poland until 1935.

The Nazi dictator, Adolf Hitler, sought to conquer all of Europe. He claimed that the Baltic seaport of Gdansk was actually German territory and that Germans who lived there were being threatened. The

Polish refusal to give up the city provided Hitler with an excuse to invade Poland. His armies invaded from the west on September 1, 1939. To make matters worse, the Soviet Union attacked from the east at the same time. During the next six years, millions of Polish citizens among many others died. Others were sent to slave labor camps in the Soviet Union and Germany.

Auschwitz was one of several German concentration camps in Poland.

Poles Resisted

Even when Russia and Germany began fighting between themselves, the situation did not improve. Yet the Poles continued to resist in their own cities and forests, as well as on battlefields in North Africa, Italy, and France. They set up a government in exile, headquartered in London. At home, the situation was desperate. Death camps were set up at Auschwitz, Treblinka, and other sites, killing Polish resistance fighters, Jews, Romanies (commonly known as Gypsies), and others. At the war's end, the country was in ruins.

After helping defeat the Germans in Poland, the Soviet Union stayed put when the war ended. A Communist government was set up in Poland. Many Polish resistance leaders were

Opposite: **German soldiers guarding a group of Polish Jews**

killed or imprisoned. The head of the Catholic Church in Poland, Stefan Cardinal Wyszynski, was also jailed. When the secret police came to arrest Wyszynski, one of them was bitten on the hand by the cardinal's dog. Before the police hauled him away, the gentle cardinal bandaged the man's wound.

Wladyslaw Gomulka

The Communist state took over some farms and businesses. Fear ruled. After a brief rebellion in 1956, some of the strictest measures were relaxed. Wladyslaw Gomulka was named head of the Polish Communist Party and instituted some reforms. The cardinal was finally freed from prison. But there was still economic repression and the threat of Soviet military intervention.

Through the 1960s and 1970s, the Poles kept up a quiet revolt. Intellectuals and workers joined forces. The Solidarity Trade Union and Lech Walesa, an electrician from the Gdansk shipyards, led the protests. There were many bloody, murderous confrontations with militia, the term used for the police during the Communist era. The economy continued to slide. Unrest spread, aided by the Church.

Cardinal Karol Wojtyla, the first Pole and the first non-Italian in hundreds of years, had been elected pope in 1978. As spiritual leader of the world's millions of Catholics, Wojtyla took the name of John Paul II. He visited his homeland in 1981, carrying a message of hope and independence.

In October 1981, the nervous Communist party met and replaced its civilian leaders with General Wojciech Jaruzelski. This concentrated all the political and military power in Poland in one man. In December of that year, Jaruzelski declared martial law. This meant the military was in full control of the country. Martial law was not lifted until 1983. Officially, the Communists were still in control. But that was only on the surface. Behind the scenes were the generals. They had organized themselves into the Military Committee for the Salvation of the Nation and a Committee of Country Defense.

Faced with deepening opposition, the Communist rulers attempted to loosen their tight control over the economy. But it was too late. By then, many people realized that the system was collapsing. They wanted a way out. In 1988, Walesa formed a

General Wojciech Jaruzelski

One of the many protests led by Lech Walesa and the Solidarity Trade Union

Citizens Committee to negotiate with the Communists. The Polish people wanted the right of free speech, legalization of Solidarity, and a free election.

Eventually, the first non-Communist government in Eastern Europe since the end of World War II was formed. Under the leadership of Mikhail Gorbachev, the Soviet Union did not interfere with this transition, much to the dismay of other Communist rulers in the area. They were afraid they would lose power. And they were right. The fall of the Polish Communists had a domino effect. Soon afterwards, Hungary, Romania, Bulgaria, Czechoslovakia, and East Germany also tossed out their dictatorial Communist rulers.

Communist Rule Ends

On December 29, 1989, the Sejm, the Polish assembly, officially ended the Poland People's Republic after forty-five years of Communist rule. The name of the country was changed to the Republic of Poland (Rzeczpospolita Polska). The Communist party dissolved itself in 1990. Nobody wanted to be a member. Some Communists joined other political parties and others formed their own organizations. Even as the Communists departed, there were many challenges remaining. But Poland was again free.

Emerging New Nation

The official name of Poland (Polska) is the Republic of Poland (Rzeczpospolita Polska). It is a democratic state. But Poland went through many political changes over the centuries. At various times, it was an independent kingdom, a vassal under the control of other nations, and a Communist dictatorship.

BEGINNING IN 1989, THE COUNTRY MOVED CAREFULLY away from totalitarianism. In this type of system, the central government controls how everything operates, often through fear and repression. This system was imposed on Poland by the Communist leaders of the Soviet Union after World War II. After the collapse of Communism, Poland has taken small but definite steps toward democracy. The Polish citizens now have a voice in running their own political affairs.

Moving away from Communism is a difficult process for almost everyone. Some Poles look back, yearning for a time when some powerful leader told them what to do. These Poles still worry a lot. They wish they could be as protected and cared for as they were years ago. But political life is not standing still in Poland. Other citizens are willing to take chances.

A car factory in Poland

Age does not make much of a difference. Most young and old Poles are already eagerly looking ahead and accepting whatever they find there. Even former Communists grudgingly admit that the "good old days" might not have been so good.

In addition to changes on the political front, Poland has been faced with other challenges. By the mid-1990s, the country moved away from Soviet economic domination. Before World War II, Poland was mostly an agricultural country. After the war, the Communists encouraged heavy industry. Polish factories produced machinery and other goods, instead of consumer items such as toasters and ironing boards. Many of these large manufactured products were sold at low prices to the Soviet Union and other Eastern European nations under Communist control.

Poles grumbled that everything seemed to be leaving Poland and nothing much was coming in. But the Communists did allow some private firms to operate. The influence and productivity of these companies grew when the political system underwent an upheaval in the late 1980s. Today, Poland is more of a trading partner with other countries. It is leaning toward the broader, more lucrative markets of Western Europe.

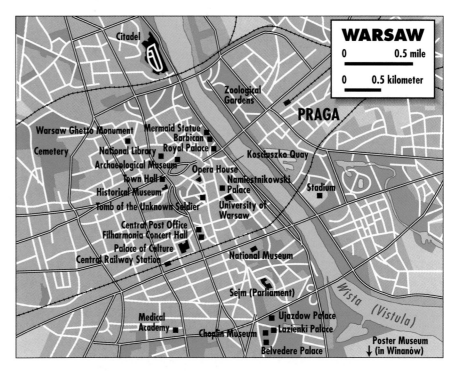

But there are still problems. To protect growing business, Poland has installed high tariffs on some goods coming into the country. A tariff is a tax placed on imports to keep them expensive, so buyers favor homemade articles.

A Capitalistic Nation

The country has also moved away from socialist policies of state-owned farms, as well as the factories, bus lines, water-works, and most other aspects of business and social services. Poland has become a capitalist nation, one now more open to a free market system of doing business. Of course, this means that not everyone is assured of a job. Some factories had to close because they were inefficient and could not compete internationally. But others are doing very well. Anyone can start a business and make a lot of money. It is estimated that more than one million new companies were formed since 1989.

Unfortunately, this is not always beneficial for everyone. There is a growing crime problem, especially with gangsters muscling in on legitimate business. Poland is also a stopover for the drug trade between the East and West. The government is trying hard to overcome these problems.

Taken on the broader spectrum, three major social shifts affected Poland during this century. The first came after World War I when Poland was finally unified after more than 120 years of being partitioned, or broken up. The next was the long period of Communist rule after World War II. The latest marks the giddy, but sometimes stumbling transition to democracy and a capitalist economic system.

New Constitution

An interim constitution was instituted in December 1992, which replaced the Communist constitution that was put into effect in 1952. The old document was backed up by guns and fear. The new document was nicknamed the "small constitution." Human rights were guaranteed, much to the relief of ordinary Poles. A new, more permanent constitution was being written in the mid-1990s.

There are many specific clauses or individual articles in the constitution. For instance, one article assigns four seats in Poland's parliament to ethnic German political parties. The Poles want to be sure that their minority citizens are also fairly represented.

The legislative branch of government consists of a two-house National Assembly (Zgromadzenie Narodowe). The first is the Senat. Two senators are chosen from each of the coun-

Constitution Day

Poland's Constitution Day is celebrated on May 3. It is a national holiday, marking the 1791 constitution that first gave the vote to many more Poles.

The Sejm building in Warsaw

Flag

The national flag of Poland has two equal horizontal stripes of white and red. The white bar is on the top, symbolizing freedom. The red bar commemorates the blood of Poland's martyrs for freedom. During the rule of Poland's kings, a white eagle was in the center of the flag.

try's forty-nine provinces. Warsaw and Katowice also have three delegates each, bringing the total of senators to 100. The other house is the Sejm and it has 460 seats. Its deputies are elected under a complex system of representation. Three hundred ninety-one members are elected from lists drawn up by parties in the country's electoral districts. The remaining sixty-nine deputies are selected from national lists. The Sejm makes the country's laws just as legislative bodies in Canada and the United States. The Senat reviews these laws and can either accept or reject them. Voters select all representatives for four-year terms.

There are forty-nine provinces or voivodships in Poland, similar to departments in France. In Polish, the plural word for these units of government is województwa. The singular term is województwo. The provinces are divided into 822 towns and 2,121 wards or *gminay*. Each province is headed by a governor. A directly elected local council helps run the provinces. Under reforms granted in 1990, the local councils have a great deal more freedom than under the old Communist system. Street repair, garbage pickup, and other such services are the council's responsibility. Poles are assessed local and national taxes to pay for these day-to-day operations.

A New Legal System

Poland's legal system is also slowly undergoing changes as the country adapts to its new democracy. There is a mixture of civil law and Communist theory. The Supreme Court, the highest legal unit in the land, is located in Warsaw. The court has the final say in appeals. It also overseas the legal system to ensure fair trials. The justices are appointed by the president, who selects them from candidates suggested by a National Council of the Judiciary.

The next level of the legal system below the Supreme Court is the administrative Supreme Court and the Court of Appeals. No jury trials were allowed under the Communists, with all decisions being made by judges. Those court officers were appointed by the government for five-year stretches. Often this was very unfair. Today, Poland is experimenting with jury trials. District courts hear civil and criminal cases. These judges are now elected.

Young people can vote when they turn eighteen years old. Many political parties try to get the voters' attention. During elections, posters are hung everywhere. Bands play at rallies. Speeches are given. Some parties are

National Anthem

Poland's national anthem is "*Jeszcze Polska nie Zginela*" ("Poland Has Not Yet Perished While We Are Still Alive"). It is sometimes called the "Dabrowski Mazurka" because it was originally an army song of the Polish Legion fighting in Italy. The legion was commanded by J. H. Dabrowski. The words to the anthem were written by Jozef Wybicki, an author, political activist, and one of the legion's organizers. He set the words to the tune of an old folk song by an unknown composer. By early in the nineteenth century, the "Dabrowski Mazurka" was considered Poland's unofficial national anthem. It gained more prominence during the revolt against the Russians in November, 1831. The tune was officially declared the anthem in 1926.

"Jeszcze Polska nie Zginela"

Poland shall not perish so long as we live.
What our enemy took from us, we'll take back
    by force.
March, march Dabrowski, from Italy to Poland
Under your command, we'll be united once more.

We will cross the Wisla and Warta rivers as
    befits loyal Poles.
Napoleon showed us how to be victorious.
March, march Dabrowski, from Italy to Poland
Under your command, we'll be united once more.

closely linked to the Solidarity Trade Union, which led the opposition to the Communist government. These parties include the Freedom Union, the Christian-National Union, Centrum, Union of Labor, Christian-Democratic Party, Conservative Party, and the Nonparty Bloc for the Support of the Reforms. However, several organizations are still tied to the old Communist way of thinking. They include the Social Democracy Party, Polish Peasants' Party, and the Democratic Left Alliance. Others are more in the middle. They range from the German Minority Party to the Union of Real Politics. Poles have many options when it comes to voting. They can pick and choose whichever organization suits their personal political interests.

The country's first free elections for all levels of government officials since World War II were held in 1990. There have been five separate Polish governments since the aftermath of Communist rule.

Lech Walesa casts his vote in the presidential election of 1990.

Poland's President

Poland is headed by a chief of state called the president of the republic. This executive is directly elected by the people for a five-year term. The president can be re-elected only once, just like the United States president. He or she is responsible for all of Poland's diplomatic affairs and can veto legislation suggested by the Sejm. But that veto can be overridden by a two-thirds vote of parliament. Lech Walesa, the former head of Solidarity, was Poland's president from 1990 until 1995, when he was voted out. Aleksander Kwásniewski, chairman of the

Socjaldezmokracja Rzeczypospolitej Polskiej (Social Democracy of the Republic of Poland), was elected in his place.

The president runs Poland with the help of a prime minister who is the actual head of government. The president appoints the prime minister from members of the cabinet, called the Council of Ministers. The ministers take care of the day-to-day direction of Poland. They head various bureaus responsible for transportation, security, culture, agriculture and other

Aleksander Kwásniewski, with his wife, was sworn in as president in 1995.

Hanna Suchocka

Hanna Suchocka was Poland's first female prime minister. She was head of the Democratic Union Party and was one of the leaders in the post-Communist Sejm. When she was a young woman, she was invited to join the Communists. Suchocka refused, saying she was to remain an independent person. She went on to be elected to parliament and was named prime minister in 1992. Faced with tough economic problems, Suchocka attempted tough remedies. She was an effective, often-praised leader, but too many Poles were not ready for her reforms. They wanted a better life immediately and did not want to patiently wait for the future. As a result, Suchocka was forced out of office. Her government collapsed, losing a vote of confidence by only one vote in the Sejm. Suchocka, however, has not given up. In the late 1990s, she remains an important opposition leader in Polish politics.

The military still has a strong presence in Poland.

affairs. The Council of Ministers is accountable to the Sejm and the president between sessions of the Sejm.

Poland still has an army. It numbers about 283,000, half of which are draftees. There are also border guards and police units, organized into special, separate services. A young person serves in the army, navy, or air force for a minimum of eighteen months. Some service personnel make the military a career and stay in much longer. If a young Pole does not wish to be placed on the draft rolls and called up for military service, he or she can be listed as a conscientious objector. This means the person then has to perform some alternative community service for three years, such as working as a teacher in a school or a hospital orderly.

Warsaw: Did You Know This?

Warsaw is Poland's capital. There are 2,316,000 residents in the city. It sprawls over 2,412 square miles (3,788 sq km). The city's symbol is a mermaid, who is half fish and half woman. This figure is armed with a sword and shield. A memorial to the siren (syrene) can be seen in the city's Kosciuszko quay (key) or harbor. According to a folktale, the mermaid princess was swimming in Vistula River and saw a handsome prince on shore. He was lost, so she sang songs while leading him to the hut of a fisherman named Wars. Wars and his wife, Sawa, greeted the prince and made him welcome, giving him directions back to his castle. Pleased that they helped, the mermaid encouraged the prince to build a city on the site of the fisherman's home and name it after them. So he did. But the city has been the Polish capital for only 401 years (1596–1997). Previously, Kraków, Poznan, and Gniezno had also served as capitals.

Warsaw's Old Market
Square

The Monument of Crosses,
one of the many memorials
in Poland

Warsaw, Poland's graceful capital, is a living symbol of everything good and bad that has happened to the country. It needed to be totally rebuilt after the destruction of World War II. On many street corners are wall plaques indicating the deaths of Polish freedom fighters killed during the war against the Nazis. One memorial marks the site of the Warsaw Ghetto. Tens of thousands of Polish Jews were imprisoned there, eventually sent to concentration or death camps. However, thousands rebelled and died during a last-ditch effort for freedom in 1943. *Child of the Warsaw Ghetto*, written by David A. Adler, tells the story of one boy who lived through that horror. Looking at all the memorials, it is as if the very streets of Warsaw still cry for these lost souls. But the city survived.

The Polish president lives in Namiestnikowski Palace on Krakowskie Przedmiescie (Square) near the Royal Castle in the historic part of Warsaw. The Palace of Culture is not far away. It was the tallest structure in the city when it was built in the 1950s. Now there are higher, modern skyscrapers nearby. Praga is a workers' suburb on the eastern bank of the Vistula

River. This area survived the war and looks much like it did a century ago. Throughout the city are open markets, where buyers can find anything from fur coats to automobile batteries and fresh carrots.

The Palace of Culture

Emerging New Nation **69**

An Economy Going in a New Direction

At the end of World War II, the Communists controlled Poland. They were backed by the military might of the Soviet army, which had driven out the Nazis with the assistance of the resistance fighters. Once their power was consolidated after threats and unfair elections in 1948, the Communists tried to wipe out the large private estates and take over small farms, but collectivization proceeded slowly. They also controlled all industry. This angered the Poles, but there was little they could do. Many Polish wartime leaders were killed or imprisoned, and the Soviet occupiers were in charge.

POLAND HAD ALWAYS BEEN AN AGRICULTURAL COUNTRY. The farms, however, were generally small and inefficient. The Communists thought they could do better. So three types of farms were established: state, collective, and private. On state farms, the farmers were paid a salary and no longer were able to plant what or when they wanted. Supposedly, the central planners had all the answers, right down to the growing season.

In collective farms, members supposedly retained ownership of the land, equipment, and livestock that they contributed to the collective when they joined. These contributions were not really voluntary, but the farmers had to go along with the law or risk losing everything to the state. On some collectives, the farmers were paid on the basis of the amount of land and material they had given to the collective. On others, they were paid according to how much work they performed.

Under the Communist system, both the state and collective farms were supposed to show the Polish peasants how productive it was to work together. But it did not turn out that way. The small holdings that remained in private hands continued to turn out more crops than all the state properties.

Polish Currency

The zloty (Zl) is the basic unit of currency of Poland. It is divided into 100 groszy. During the early 1990, Poland experienced extremely high inflation rates. At one point in 1994, 24,000 zloties were equal to U.S. $1. In January 1995, the Polish government instituted a currency reform; 10,000 old zloties were replaced with one new zloty. The exchange rate in 1997 was 3.16 zloties to the U.S.$1.

Protests Continue

By the early 1950s, it was obvious that the state farms were not working. Farmers on the state farms and collectives kept protesting. Most got their land back and were able to again concentrate on taking care of their livestock, instead of worrying about politics. By the mid-1980s, some 85 percent of the farms was owned and worked by individual peasant families. The remainder were owned by corporations.

Farmers protested the state-run farms and eventually got their land back.

Today's Polish farms are small compared with the vast acres planted in Canada's western provinces or in the Great Plains of the United States. The average Polish farm is only 12 acres (5 ha). While many still use horses to pull equipment, modern technology is making inroads on the traditional

ways of doing things. Mechanized plows, tractors, and threshing machines are now more often seen lumbering across the fields. But it not unusual to see a horse-drawn cart in a major city, bringing farm produce to market.

Despite their size, the farms are very productive. They are among the world's largest producers of potatoes, vegetables, and fruit. Polish beef is also world famous for its quality. The opening of new markets in Western Europe has helped the Polish farmer. Rye, barley, sugar beets, clover, and alfalfa are important commodities.

Yet Poland cannot supply all its food needs. It still needs to import flour from Canada and France. Kazakhstan and Canada supply durum wheat used in making bread. The United States has a hard time cracking this market because it cannot compete with the lower prices and trade agreements made between Poland and some other nations.

Horse-drawn carts have often been replaced by tractors.

Poland is branching out from traditional farming to other agricultural ventures. Production of forest products is increasing, as the country takes advantage of its timber resources. Wood is used for many products, from furniture to wafer board. As the trees are harvested, seedlings are planted to replace them. This ensures an ongoing crop. Growing tobacco is another important farming industry. It is estimated that 14 million Poles smoke more than 120 billion cigarettes annually. Most are produced in seven state-run factories. This lucrative market is enviously eyed by the United States tobacco companies and those from other nations. Under licensing agreements, several international companies have been given permission to produce an additional 46 billion cigarettes.

The timber industry has grown in Poland.

The mining industry in Poland is very important to the national economy. The Ministry of Industry and Trade oversees the country's mining and energy sectors. This is an important responsibility because Poland is ranked fourth in the world for its coal production. Silesia in southeastern Poland is called the "Black Country" and is known for its deep mines. This giant coal basin stretches for miles across the surface of the ground and extends up to 2 miles (3.2 km) underground. The mines near the city of

Katowice produce high-quality anthracite coal. It is used to fuel the country's sprawling steel mills of Nowa Huta, an industrial complex in the Kraków suburbs. The plants, warehouses, and shipping facilities here are one of the largest concentrations of heavy industry in Europe. Softer coal is also shipped from Poland to foundries in the Czech Republic and Slovakia.

Coal Reserves

There are still large reserves of the various kinds of Polish coal. So, the long-term prospects for mining remain good. The World Bank, which keeps an eye on these things, predicts a tripling of world energy consumption through the year 2030. As a result, Poland's coal will be in demand for years to come. Polish coal fuels 95 percent of its own industrial plants. But many factories need refurbishment and updating to met new standards of technology. The World Bank and Poland signed an agreement in 1991 for a loan of $1.3 billion to finance these renovations and the construction

Coal is one of the materials mined.

Long-term prospects for coal mining remain good in Poland.

of new facilities. It is expected that this will keep Poland competitive on the world market.

The construction of a gas pipeline from the northern Russian district of Siberia to Western Europe will bring another source of fuel to Poland. The pipeline runs for 2,480 miles (4,000 km) and cost $35 billion to build. The Polish section of the pipeline is one of the largest construction projects ever undertaken in the country. It is to become operational in 1999.

What Poland Grows, Makes, and Mines	
Agriculture *(value of production in Zl'000,000,000; 1993)*	
Potatoes	26,237
Wheat	19,220
Rye	8,243
Sugar beets	6,845
Manufacturing *(value of production in Zl'000,000,000; 1993)*	
Food	293,206
Machinery and transport equipment	279,797
Chemicals	121,030
Mining *(in millions of metric tons; 1993)*	
Electrolytic copper	404,000
Zinc	150,400
Lead	54,000
Aluminum	46,900

For centuries, Polish salt has also been in great demand. The salt mines of Wieliczka, 7 miles (11 km) from Kraków, descend 442 feet (135 m) below the surface. Mining has gone on here for more than 1,000 years. Deep underground are miles of tunnels and caverns. There are even volleyball and tennis courts, as well as a hospital for miners. In the seventeenth century, a chapel was carved out of the salt. Statues and murals made of salt peer down from the high walls. During World War II, the Nazis had an aircraft plant hidden in the mines, far beyond reach of enemy bombs.

Poland is also known for its salt mines.

When the Communists moved into power, they eagerly sought to build more heavy industrial plants. This brought many workers in to the city from the rural areas. All the planning was centralized, with state managers determining what would be produced and when. This was not very efficient. When Communism changed to the more freewheeling type of market economy in the 1990s, however, it was hard on Polish workers. Many were not prepared for competition. After all, a generation was assured of a job and added bonuses, such as long vacations. While some businesspeople and workers still make out very well, a large number have yet to see the benefits of a more open economic system. This has led to the fall of several post-Communist governments.

A modern shopping center

Small Industries

After the collapse of the Communist economic system, numerous small industries sprang up. Some started under the old regime and were able to blossom after tight government controls were lifted. One business that did very well was the Dana Noble Ceramics Company, which was established in 1975. The company has 350 different artistic patterns used for its bowls, jugs, mugs, tea and coffee sets, plates, vases, ceramic chandeliers, clay figures, plate clocks, and incense-burning lamps. Other eager entrepreneurs started furniture factories, launched high fashion clothing lines, and opened computer outlets. Not all such ventures are successful but savvy Poles continue to eagerly try new ventures.

Thousands of manufactured goods are stamped with the "Made in Poland" tag. Polish shirts are worn in Zaire. Polish cement is used to build highways and dams in China, Ghana, and Egypt. Polish folding canoes and waterproof tents are used by campers in Spain. Endless stretches of Polish steel railroad rails crisscross Brazil. Automobiles assembled in Poland are driven on highways in India. Cities such as Poznan are noted for their industrial muscle; factories produce ball bearings, rubber products, ship engines, instant coffee, crankshafts, and cereal.

Although Poland has many natural resources, sometimes there are not enough raw materials to produce all the goods that buyers want. Therefore, iron ore is imported from Russia and other Eastern European nations. Polish factories then can make pig iron, rolled steel, and other materials for resale.

Opposite: **U.S. companies have a presence in Poland.**

Primary Land Use

▨	Farming, livestock
▨	Wheat
☐	Cereals, potatoes
▨	Forests

Industry and Resources

▨	Industrial area	K	Potash
C	Coal	Lg	Lignite
Cu	Copper	Na	Salt
Fe	Iron ore	O	Oil
G	Natural gas	Zn	Zinc

In order of importance, Poland's major trading partners are Germany, the United Kingdom, the Czech Republic, Slovakia, Austria, United States, the Netherlands, and France. But there is an imbalance of trade, a fact that Poland would like to reverse. An imbalance means that more goods come into the country than are sold outside the nation. For a time, Poland spent more than it made. This created a huge debt. Poland once owed more than

A train station in Warsaw

$4 billion to the United States. But after long, careful negotiations with Western banks, much of the debt load was reduced in 1994. This helped stimulate the Polish economy, so it is hoped the market will even out.

The economic changes in Poland put additional stress on the country's infrastructure. Its roads, bridges, rail lines, and airports had to be expanded and improved. They needed to meet the demands of growing trade and transportation. In the late 1980s, about 50 percent of the country's highways required repair. Another 30 percent were classified as in poor shape. But between 1996 and 2011, more than 1,550 miles (2,500 km) of new highways will be built. Poland's railway system is the third largest in Europe, with 16,120 miles (26,000 km) of track. However, much of its rolling equipment, from engines to freight cars, also needs refurbishment. Loans for this work are coming from the World Bank and the European Union, a group of European nations.

Poland's rivers are important in moving freight. The country has 2,400 miles (4,000 km) of navigable waterways on which barges and tugs can operate. There is always plenty of dockside hustle and bustle in Warsaw along the Vistula, in Wroclaw on the Oder River, and in Gliwice on the Kanal

Gliwicki. Huge freighters sailing under dozens of national flags berth at the major seaports of Gdansk, Gdynia, Szczecin, and Swinoujscie. They import, or bring in, loads of chemicals and heavy equipment, as well as consumer goods. On their way back out to sea, the freighters carry out Polish-grown food and locally made machinery. There are 209 airports in Poland, with 70 large enough to serve international passengers and freight haulers.

Harbor Crane

Gdansk's towering wooden Harbor Crane was built in the fifteenth century. The crane loaded goods on sailing vessels for many years. Today, the old structure brings alive centuries of Poland's economic connection with the outside world. Long retired from active use, it now houses the city's Maritime Museum and is packed with artifacts.

Businesspeople face several difficulties in Poland. Inflation is one problem, an economic problem whereby money quickly loses its value. A slow, sometimes inefficient, banking system is another. Also, the telecommunication system in Poland needs a major overhaul. In the mid-1990s, only ten of every hundred Poles had a telephone. But that fact is slowly changing, with the number of phones growing by 12 percent a year. Digital cellular networks are also being established. Poles carry their handheld cellular phones, just as their overseas cousins in Canada and the United States. In fact, there is a new law in Poland prohibiting their use while driving!

The Polish people have begun to use cellular phones.

Foreign investment is needed and appreciated by Poland's economic leaders, but international investors must conform to Polish laws. For instance, a non-Polish company can lease

Poland has twenty-seven AM radio stations and twenty-seven FM stations. These private carriers broadcast news, music, and talk shows, as in Canada and the United States. There are forty television stations. In addition to Polish programs, listeners and viewers can watch shows from around Europe.

Poland is the seventh-largest cable user in Europe, with more than a million customers. Children can even watch MTV.

Newspapers and magazines remain popular, since Poles are avid readers. There are about eighty daily newspapers in Poland, plus weeklies, sports journals, ladies' magazines, and other publications.

farmland for a maximum of ninety-nine years. When Communism collapsed, outside investors felt better about putting their money into Polish projects. Yet, sometimes, outside companies have had a hard time getting used to the Polish way of life and doing business. One large baby-food manufacturer from the United States opened a factory in Poland, thinking it would make millions of dollars by selling its high-priced processed foods. But young Polish moms preferred to make less-expensive, more tasty food themselves for their children.

Poland does not take money and goods from the outside world without giving anything back. The country's highly educated engineers and skillful construction workers are in great demand, especially in developing Third World countries. These professionals share their expertise in manufacturing, building trades, and design.

Approximately 18 million Poles are employed. About 40 percent are in farming and 35 percent are in trade and manufacturing. The others work for the government and transportation companies or in communications. More jobs are opening in the textile, fuel, power, timber, and food-processing industries. Financial and insurance industries are attracting larger numbers of young Poles, because they can use their newly learned computer skills. In fact, the computer industry is exploding for both business and personal use. In 1995, for the first time, Poland allowed its citizens to deduct the purchase of computer equipment from their taxes.

A blacksmith practicing his craft

Young Country

Poland is a relatively young country, at least in terms of its citizens' age since millions of an earlier generation were killed in World War II. It would have been as if everyone over thirty living in Toronto, Vancouver, Calgary, Montreal, San Francisco, Dallas, Miami, and Denver had died, leaving only their children. These young Polish workers are well aware of the need to compete effectively in a worldwide market system. A national labor code regulates employee-worker relations and ensures everyone's rights and duties. Labor unions have always been strong in the country. Remember the momentous impact that the Solidarity Trade Union had in bringing down Poland's former repressive political system.

Except for farmers, who have to tend their livestock at all hours, the average workday runs from 8 A.M. to 5 P.M. It is important to have a big breakfast because few workers take time off for lunch. They often have a break in the middle of the afternoon. They eat supper after work and have a light snack later in the evening. Many workers are also on the job on weekends, although they usually get Saturday afternoons off and have the day's main meal around 1 P.M.

The average family eats dinner together in the early evening.

Today, people work because they have an investment in their business and more of a personal stake in making their country competitive and successful. That often makes the hard labor seem to go easier.

An Economy Going in a New Direction **83**

Wonders of the Polish People

Fifteen hundred years ago, Roman legionnaires patrolled the far-northern borders of the empire. These tough veterans of countless ancient wars often encountered wandering tribes of hunters and warriors. These were the Slavs. Because the Slavs had different customs and were beyond the empire's frontier, the Romans called them barbarians.

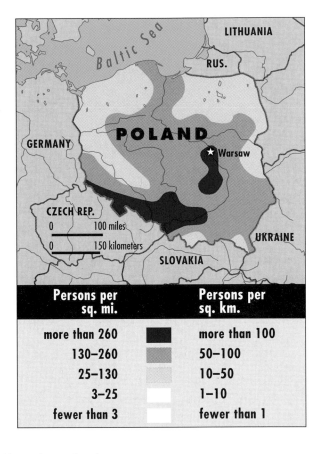

Persons per sq. mi.

more than 260	(black)
130–260	(dark gray)
25–130	(light gray)
3–25	(white)
fewer than 3	(white)

Persons per sq. km.

more than 100	
50–100	
10–50	
1–10	
fewer than 1	

T HE UNRULY SLAVS WERE FIERCE FIGHTERS, striking out of their forested hideaways at Roman patrols. They could then hide out in the thick woods, out of reach in their mountain strongholds. The Romans were never able to conquer these hit-and-run warriors. They were happy just to keep them out of the territories Rome already controlled. Occasionally, prisoners were taken. The word slave originally meant a captive seized from this Slavic region of northern Europe. Then, as the Roman empire declined, the Slavs moved out from their original lands to seek new territory.

By the fifth century, the Polabians, or Elbe Slavs, had settled along the Elbe River. Near them were the Lusatain Slavs, or Wends. The Pomeranians were Slavs living along the Baltic Coast. They all established fortified camps, which evolved into some of the most notable cities of northern and eastern Europe. Other Slavs traveled over the rugged Carpathian Mountains into what is now Slovakia and the Czech Republic. More Slavs went as far south as today's Balkan countries. Still others went east into Russia. Each of these groups gradually developed their own traditions and customs, yet their basic language remained relatively the same. They battled other ethnic groups for land and cattle. Among their enemies was a Celtic tribe called the Boii, forerunners of the Bohemians.

Gniezno

There are two folktales that tell how Poland came to be. They each involve three brothers who led the Slavs on their journey across northern Europe. They stopped to rest in a land that the storytellers said was very beautiful. In the first story, Lech, one of the brothers, saw a white eagle land in a tree. He considered this a good omen so he decided to stay in that spot. This area eventually became Poland. The white eagle remains the country's symbol.

The other folktale says that during his wanderings, Lech found a bird nest in a high tree. He climbed the tree and look all around the countryside, falling in love with the wide plains, rushing streams, and mountains. He took this to mean he should settle down and live in that area. Lech called his new home Gniezno (Gnyez-no), which means nest. According to the legend, this became the first town in Poland. There still is a famous city in Poland called Gniezno. It is interesting to note that Solidarity Trade Union leader Lech Walesa had the same name as the folktale founder of old Poland. Walesa and his supporters help create a new Poland in the 1980s and 1990s through their revolutionary activities.

But the brothers of that first Lech, Czech and Rus, were eager to move on. They wanted even more space. With his family and friends, Rus meandered east into what is now Russia and settled there. Czech and his tribe went south to the mountains of what would be the Czech Republic on today's maps.

As it turns out, these legends of Poland's founding are close to reality. Three distinct Slavic tribes actually were the long-ago ancestors of today's Poles, Czechs, and Russians.

Polanie Settle Down

The Polanie, which means dwellers on the plain, were one of the largest of the major Slavic clans. After centuries of moving about, the Polanie found that the best places to live were along the banks of Poland's many rivers. From here, the Polanie could easily use the waterways to move crops, furs, and other goods to neighboring villages for trade. They became farmers, fishers and merchants. During these long years, the strongest warriors began to call themselves princes and set up a rule of power and law. Each prince made his home in a fort called a *grod*. Many important Polish cities such as Poznan grew out of these early settlements.

But pockets of smaller Slavic clans remained scattered throughout the territories of the larger groups. A few people in modern Poland still speak ancient dialects and keep their own customs. Among them are Kaszubians from the Baltic coast and Jatzvigians of central Poland. In the late 1800s, thousands of Kaszubian fishers emigrated to the United States. Many settled along the western rim of Lake Michigan, whose broad blue waters reminded them of their turbulent, but beloved, Baltic Sea. These arrivals added a colorful new ethnic flavor to such cities as Milwaukee, which already had a large Polish emigrant population. In America, as in Poland, the Kaszubians were great fishers.

Poznan is known for being one of Poland's prettiest cities.

The arrival of the Huns

A Corpus Christi procession

Many Invaders

Even as the Polanie evolved into the Poles, great waves of humanity continually migrated across Poland from the East and from the West. The lack of natural borders allowed the Huns, Avars, and Goths to rampage over the fertile plains of this long-ago Poland. They each left a bit of their culture behind, all of which was absorbed by an all-encompassing Polish vitality.

As an example, on the feast of Corpus Christi in Kraków, a man dressed in a turban and flowing robes runs through the crowds partying in the city center. Riding a giant toy rocking horse, he swings a great whip around his head. The man hits the revelers with large, soft balls tied to the ends of the whip. Laughing and cheering, everybody pushes and shoves him back. At the end of his ride through the city square, the man is treated to a huge dinner. It is an honor to be chosen for this event. But the pageant brings to mind when the fierce Tatars captured and looted Kraków in 1241. The honoree can usually trace his ancestors back to the original defenders of the city.

One distinct group of ancient people living in northern and eastern Poland were the Prussians, a pagan Germanic tribe. They were especially numerous along the Baltic Coast.

As they evolved as a nationality, the Prussians remained proud of their heritage and remained aloof from their Polish neighbors. They were known for their military bearing. In fact, Prussian General Frederick Von Steuben helped train and discipline America's colonial army toward the end of the Revolutionary War.

An independent kingdom before 1871, the territory of Prussia became the center around which the mighty German Empire was formed. Over the centuries, the presence of the Prussians was a continual problem for Poland. This all came to a tragic, bloody conclusion in the 1930s. Nazi dictator Adolf Hitler said he wanted to protect the rights of these Germanic people. He claimed the Poles were unfairly treating the Prussians as second-class citizens and that the Poles had no right to a sea corridor that divided Germany. This gave him an excuse to invade Poland in 1939, an act that launched the World War II.

Failed Tactics

Every other invader of Poland also attempted to put his own foreign stamp on the Polish people. Almost all the conquerors even forbade Poles to sing in their own language. This tactic failed when the people switched to Latin and continued to sing their same folk tunes and hymns. In the mid-nineteenth century, Chancellor Wilhelm von Bismarck tried to germanize the areas of Poland under his control. Bismarck was a Prussian and had no love for Poles. Even though he crushed a Polish revolution in 1863, Bismarck's efforts were rebuffed

Frederick Von Steuben

Who Lives in Poland?

Polish	98%
Ukranian	1%
German/Belarussian	0.8%
Jewish	0.1%
Other	0.1%

Population of Major Polish Cities

Warsaw	2,316,000
Lodz (1992 est.)	842,300
Kraków (1992 est.)	751,500
Wroclaw	642,900
Poznan (1992 est.)	589,300
Gdansk (1992 est.)	466,700

Traditional dress of Poland

almost everywhere else. But he was shrewd and crafty. He allowed his Polish male subjects to marry German women. But it was forbidden for a German man to marry a Polish woman. He said that the Polish woman would bring her child up as a Pole, regardless of the nationality of her husband. This decree did not last long. Polish men did not like being told what to do by an outsider, much less a Prussian outsider. No one paid any attention to the law and it was soon dropped.

Throughout all those troubled years, Poles kept their heads high and retained their sense of identity. Each district of Poland also kept its distinctive customs, most notably with clothing. Colorful costumes are often handed down from generation to generation as family heirlooms. During holidays, girls who live near Poznan still stroll around the city wearing dark skirts, which are covered with long, white lace vests. In other parts of Poland, women wear kerchiefs on their heads, while Poznan's ladies wear large white hats tied with lace ribbons around their chins to celebrate.

The traditional trouser is hand-woven and embroidered.

Colorful Clothing

In the villages around the weaving center of Lowicz, the skirts have many different colors. Even Polish men have distinctive clothing. Herders in the Carpathian Mountains wear richly embroidered vests and tight, white trousers woven from goat hair. Their small felt hats have headbands adorned with tiny seashells.

Polish cities also have their characteristic dress. Each community has an individual architectural style.

Architecture

Because of their interesting architecture, some Polish towns seem to belong somewhere else. Several have the look of Turkish cities with tall towers called minarets. Others appear Russian, with onion-domed roofs on the public buildings. Zamosc appears to be an Italian town. The city was the idea of Jan Zamoyski, the Italian-educated chancellor of Poland under sixteenth-century King Stefan Batory (below). Zamoyski wanted to build a perfect town, one that would become Poland's trading center. So he hired Bernardo Morando, an architect from Padua, Italy, to design the official buildings and merchant palaces. Paintings in the local basilica were

done by the son of the famed artst Tintoretto, who was from Venice, Italy. Zamosc (right) is so beautiful that it is classified by UNESCO as a special historical site of worldwide significance.

Wilanow Palace in Warsaw

Polish communities are no strangers to the terrible fate of urban renewal by warfare. Over the centuries, they were always damaged during wars. Sandomierz, a town on the Vistula River, was destroyed twice by the Tatars and rebuilt and destroyed again by the Swedes. It was then heavily damaged during World War II. But with their keen sense of history, the Poles rebuilt Sandomierz and other cities carefully so that they look much like they did generations ago.

Elegant Warsaw

Warsaw was also considered to be one of the most elegant cities of Europe, with its castles, public buildings, theaters, and palaces. But 90 percent of Warsaw was leveled during World War II. During the final days of the fighting in 1945, the Nazis

destroyed the city. They blew up block by block until only vast piles of rubble remained. They killed any resistance fighters and civilians they found.

The Soviet army was close enough to save the city and its citizens. But it refused to do so until the Nazis abandoned their positions. The Soviets then marched in, claiming credit for liberating Warsaw. It took years for the Poles to rebuild their capital, but they did. Using old plans, photographs, drawings, and lots of hard work and dedication, the Old City (Stare Miasto) was reborn on the east bank of the Vistula River. Around the city, the rebuilders incorporated many memorials and monuments to all the dead patriots. On the west bank is modern Warsaw, with skyscrapers, housing projects, and factories. Poland is a country that refuses to give up.

A Religious People

Religion is part of everyday life for most Poles. Even if a person does not attend church regularly, the role the Church has played in Polish history is a constant. Faith is strongest in the countryside, where traditions and old lifestyles are slow to change. Farmers often begin their day with prayers. They stop at noon to offer another prayer.

Спаси
Господі
люди
вдя
бла
зослові
состо
пнаство
сен крес
постав-

Churches are kept open, so people can use them at any time of day.

THERE ARE MANY ROADSIDE SHRINES IN the Polish countryside. It is not unusual to see a passerby stop near one and make the sign of the cross. If the shrine honors Jesus Christ, the person might kiss the statue's feet. Even in the cities, the doors to churches are always open. The buildings provide a quiet place to pray and reflect throughout the day. Votive candles flicker in the low light and the scent of incense sweetens the air. A few people always seem to be kneeling or sitting in each church. Some older Poles still give their ages by referring to the closest saint's day or religious holiday. For instance, a person might indicate, "After last Assumption Day, I was ninety years old."

When a guest enters a house, parents say, "When there is a guest in the home, God is in the home." The visitor replies, "Praised be Jesus Christ" ("Nieck bedzie pochwalony Jezus Chrystus" or "Nyek benje pokvalony Yesus Krystoos"). The family then responds by saying, "Forever and ever, Amen." One of Poland's leading philosophers, Leszek Kolakowski, is an atheist, a person who doesn't believe in God. However, when Kolakowski met Pope John Paul II at a conference in Italy, the

Pope John Paul II

Pope John Paul II is the first Polish pope, the spiritual leader of the world's millions of Roman Catholics. For 500 years, the pope was always an Italian, so when Cardinal Karol Wojtyla was crowned pope, a hush seemed to fall on the country as everyone watched the event on television.

Karol Jozef Wojtyla *(above left)* was born in the village of Wadowice on May 18, 1920. His parents were poor and his mother died when he was only nine years old. Wojtyla was a good student who excelled in history, math, Latin, and Polish. When he was twenty-one years old, his father died. Wojtyla was forced to quit school and go to work in a stone quarry and a chemical factory. During this time, he decided to become a priest and went to live in the Archbishop's Palace in Kraków. After more coursework and ordination, which is the ceremony for becoming a priest, he went to Rome and studied at the Angelicum University to finish his degree in theology. He went on to teach religion and became the auxiliary bishop of Kraków in 1958. Six years later, Wojtyla became archbishop. He eventually was made a cardinal, one of the highest positions in the Roman Catholic Church, in 1970.

His predecessor, Pope John Paul I, died in 1978 and a new pope had to be elected. Other cardinals from around the world then journeyed to Vatican City, where the Roman Catholic Church is headquartered. After much deliberation, Wojtyla was selected, taking the name of Pope John Paul II *(below left)*. The cardinals agreed he was the best clergyman for the job. The pope made several trips to Poland throughout the years, even when his homeland was under Communist rule. While the government would have preferred not to have him visit, they could not do anything about it. The Poles are very proud of "their" pope.

Polish-born pope greeted him with the same welcome he does to followers of the Church. The philosopher did not mind. After all, he was Polish and understood the tradition.

The primary religion in Poland remains Roman Catholicism, which became the country's official religion in 966. This was when Mieszko I, Poland's first king, was baptized. But it was not until the early 1200s before the numerous pagan tribes of Poland finally adopted Christianity. The country's patron saint, Stanislaw, was canonized, or made a saint, in 1253. The ceremony was important because it drew Poles together from all over the country. It was one of the first times that the nobility, the clergy, and the laypeople were united. Even after the country was broken up or ruled by outsiders years later, the Church remained the single constant that kept the national spirit of Poland alive.

Stanislaw, the patron saint of Poland

Polish churches can be very ornate.

Catholic Poles

Today, at least 95 percent of Poles indicate they are Catholic. Even those do not regularly attend Sunday services say they are proud of the Church's traditions. Of course, there are other Christian denominations in Poland. But they have a smaller percentage of followers, less than 5 percent of the population. Of these the largest is the Russian Orthodox Church, with about 100,000 members who mostly live in eastern Poland. Even smaller numbers belong to three Old Catholic denominations that are not affiliated with the

Religions of Poland

Roman Catholic	90.5%
Orthodox Christian	1.5%
Protestant Christian	less than 1%
Islam	less than 1%
Judaism	less than 1%

A Polish girl dressed for her First Communion

The ceremony of blessing of the fields is usually held the Monday after Easter.

official Catholic Church. Some people, many of German heritage, belong to several Protestant denominations. They are primarily Lutherans and members of the Evangelist-Reform Church. There are also Jews and some Moslems.

The Church itself and religious orders of priests and nuns operate their own schools for younger pupils, augmenting the public school system. The Catholic Church also oversees the Lublin Catholic University and the Academy of Catholic Theology in Warsaw.

Unquestioned Authority

The parish priest is the most important person in a village. His authority is usually unquestioned, especially in the countryside. In the spring, he blesses the earth to ensure good crops. He presides at weddings, funerals, and baptisms. He is recognized for his education and his insights on life. The local church is the center of the community's social, as well as

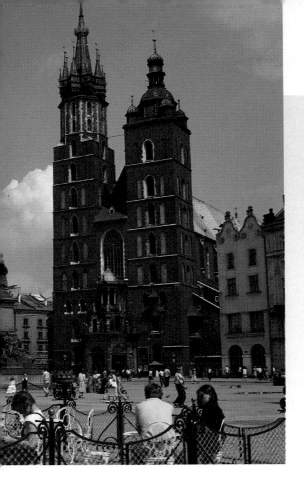

Church of Saint Mary

There are many folktales surrounding the Church of Saint Mary (Kosciol Mariacki) in Kraków. The building has two towers of unequal height. According to legend, the towers were built by two brothers. One worked fast, with great care for craftsmanship. The other brother was slower. The slower man was jealous that his brother was finishing the job more quickly. So he murdered his brother with a sword. But the murderer was so sorry for the deed, he jumped from his tower and killed himself. So the towers remain of different heights today. The weapon that supposedly was used in the killing now hangs in the city's Cloth Hall, an old building where merchants gathered.

In the thirteenth century, more tragedy struck. When Kraków was attacked by the Tatars, a bugler in one of the church towers sounded an alarm. He was killed by an arrow, silencing his warning cries. To this day, every hour on the hour, a modern bugler trumpets four times at the church. He suddenly ends the melody on the same note as did the hero trumpeter. This reminds city residents of the bravery of that soldier long ago.

spiritual life. Common worship binds the congregation into a tightly knit group. This is one of the reasons invaders have always had trouble conquering the proud Poles.

Many Poles in the countryside still wear their colorful national costumes to church. They enjoy showing off their intricate embroidery and sewing skills. There is always a lot of singing and fiddling after services, with dances in the church yard after mass. Provincial towns (called *powiat*) have larger churches. A monsignor, who is higher in the ecclesiastical order than a village priest, usually is head of a city parish.

Holidays in Poland

New Year's Day	January 1
Easter Monday	
Labour Day	May 1
Polish National Day	May 3
Victory Day	May 9
Corpus Christi	
Assumption	August 15
All Saints' Day	November 1
Independence Day	November 11
Christmas	December 25

The history of the Polish Catholic Church has always been stormy. When the Church came to Poland, it placed the land under the protection of the Germanic Holy Roman Empire. In the tenth century, the pope recognized Germany as the successor to the ancient Roman Empire. This placed Poland in the Western European sphere of influence, not in that of Russia and its Eastern European traditions. This German connection has often led to trouble for Poland because Germany has been among the long list of countries to invade Poland over the years. Often, the Church remained the only protector of the Polish people.

The history of the Jews and Catholics in Poland is also closely related. For ten centuries, the two cultures were intertwined. The beginnings of Polish Catholicism years ago was related in stories written by a Jewish amber dealer named Ibrahim Ibn-Jakub. He lived in the city of Gniezno near Warsaw, home of Poland's first bishop and the residence of the country's cardinal primate, the highest church authority in today's Poland. Ibn-Jakub's observations provided deep insights into the Church's earliest days. Later, in the reign of King Mieszko II, the Hebrew word for peace, *shalom*, was engraved on silver coins.

There were Jewish residents in even the most remote Polish villages. Each Jewish community was governed by a committee of scholars and religious leaders, called a *kahal*. All the kahals were subject to the Council of Four Lands, modeled after the

Polish Sejm, the national parliament. This was the only Jewish parliament that ever existed outside of Israel.

The Jews formed the business backbone of many Polish communities. They founded businesses and expanded trade. They were the bankers who loaned money. They were the tailors, bakers, and other skilled artisans. They were also numbered in the cultural elite. Their music, literary works, and drama are included in the best of Poland's rich tapestry of traditions. They were great soldiers. Colonel Berek Joselewicz became a Polish national hero fighting during the 1794 revolution. There is even a plum brandy made in southern Poland that is called Pejsachowka. Jewish residents of the area gave the drink its name many years ago. They drank the brandy during holiday of Passover (Pejsach).

In many countries, however, anti-Semitism, or hatred of Jews, is a problem. Even Poland was not exempt. Some misguided people have always found it convenient to blame their difficulties on the Jews. This hostility peaked during World War II.

When the Nazis marched into Poland into World War II, they rounded up the Jews and took them to concentration camps to be killed. Some non-Jewish Poles, such as Tadeusz Pankiewicz, a brave pharmacist in Kraków, protected their Jewish neighbors as best they could. They fed them, hid

A Jewish summer camp in 1930. Many Jews had regular lives in Poland before World War II.

A Jewish cemetery

them, or helped the Jews escape the county. There were many such heroes. Before the Holocaust, there were 3.5 million Jews in Poland. Fewer than 4,000 Jews live here today. Even after the war, the Communists continued to blame the Jews for many of the country's woes. Synagogues, schools, and other Jewish centers remain in decay or have been turned to other uses. A housing project covers the site of the Warsaw Ghetto, where thousands of Jews died fighting their Nazi oppressors.

Church Resistance

After World War II, the Church provided the main resistance to the Communists who were atheists. During martial law, prior to the collapse of the Communist system, church buildings provided a safe haven for Solidarity activists. The priests and nuns fought alongside their fellow citizens. Their education of young people kept the spirit of freedom and Polish history alive. Several clergy were killed in the struggle and were known as martyrs to the cause.

The Blessed Mother, the mother of Jesus Christ, is revered by the Poles. Each year, more than a million pilgrims come to the Jasna Gora Monastery near Czestochowa. Inside the building is a painting called the Black Madonna, which is said to cause miracles. This is the most sacred place in Poland, where people gather to see the unveiling twice daily of the portrait of their Virgin.

While the Church remains a strong force in the new Poland, it does not have quite the same power as it did previ-

Father Maximilian Kolbe

Father Maximilian Kolbe *(left)* was canonized a saint in the Catholic Church in 1982. This is the highest honor given to anyone in the Church, meaning that the person is officially recognized as pre-eminent in holiness. Kolbe voluntarily took the place of a prisoner in the Dachau concentration camp when the guards need one more prisoner to fill their quota of those be killed that day. The man saved by Kolbe's bravery was still alive in the 1990s.

Kolbe carried on the tradition of Saint Adalbert (Saint Wojciech), Poland's first saint. Adalbert was murdered by the pagans he was trying to convert to Christianity. Twelve bronze panels on the door of the Gniezno Cathedral *(below)* depict his life and death.

ously. People are beginning to question the clergy's authority. Years ago, birth control and abortion would not even be discussed. Today, these and other important issues dealing with people's lives are being discussed. Regardless of these changing times, however, Poles continue to agree that their country would have been lost without the role played by Church over the centuries.

The Black Madonna icon at Jasna Gora Monastery

Colorful Poland

East shakes hands with West in the Polish arts world. In its earliest days, Poland's vibrant cultural life was influenced by all the people who crisscrossed the Polish frontier. Travelers told of new ideas and ways of doing things. Merchants brought goods from exotic lands. The royalty and wealthy surrounded themselves the cultural elite from many lands. Their deep pocketbooks also supported homegrown talent as well. The Poles took the best of all these influences, complementing them with their own artistic experiences.

Bᴜᴛ Pᴏʟɪsʜ ᴄᴜʟᴛᴜʀᴇ ʜᴀs ᴀʟsᴏ ʙᴇᴇɴ sʜᴀᴘᴇᴅ ʙʏ ᴛʜᴇ violence, horror, and upheaval afflicting the country for hundreds of years. The flowers of Poland's intellectual world were often earmarked for death or imprisonment. Usually, their crimes seemed minor. As one example, poet Adam Mickiewicz was one of Poland's many literary greats exiled in the mid-1800s. He was punished for writing about wrong-headed nationalism. It made no difference who the oppressor was.

Adam Mickiewicz

Sense of Pride

Architecture, music, painting, drama, and literature have long been vibrant parts of Polish life—despite being often overrun and trampled by foreigners. This is readily evident when

Henryk Sienkiewicz, with his children

reading works by such Polish authors as Wladyslaw Reymont. In 1924, he won a Nobel Prize in literature for his story about Polish farm life called *The Peasants.* Henryk Sienkiewicz, another Nobel Prize winner, wrote *Quo Vadis,* an earlier epic novel about Christianity and

Czeslaw Milosz

Wislawa Szymborska

the Roman Empire. Sienkiewicz won his award in 1905 and went on to write many other works. A third Polish writer, poet Czeslaw Milosz, also won the Nobel Prize. His award was given in 1980 for a lifetime of verse. Many of his contemporary works rapped the Communist system. In 1996, Polish poet Wislawa Szymborska also won the Nobel Prize in literature. Her most famous works include *People on a Bridge* (1990) and *View with a Grain of Sand* (1995).

Famous Polish Jews, such as Sholom Aleichem and Isaac Peretz, wrote classic tales of Jewish life in Poland. They wrote in Yiddish, a mixture of Hebrew, German, and Polish.

Jerzy Harasymowicz is one of the most famous modern poets in modern Poland. Many of his children's poems feature a haiku-like verse. Their compact, lyrical style is easy and fun to read. The poem "I Live on a Raft" focuses on fantasy worlds that kids can enjoy. "All summer long, my houseboat floats through the clouds" where "now and then, airplanes like dolphins play tag with me and then disappear," he writes. Ewa Zadrzynska's *Peaceable Kingdom* is a wonderful children's story about animals in a painting that come to life. She now lives in the United States.

Spirit Carried Abroad

Polish authors carried their feisty literary spirit abroad wherever they traveled. Joseph Conrad (Josef Teodor Konrad Nalecz Korzeniowski) spoke Polish and French by the time he was five years old. He learned several more languages as a merchant seaman. Conrad put aside his native Polish and took up writing in English when he was in his forties. *Heart of Darkness* and *Lord Jim* were among his most famous books. Other famous authors who made names for themselves outside Poland include children's book writer Uri Shulevitz. As a youngster, he escaped from the terrors of the Warsaw Ghetto during World War II.

Joseph Conrad

Poland is also famous for its theater. Everyone loves the bright lights of the stage, when the curtain rises and the audience hushes. Jewish actress Esther Rachel Kaminska, who lived from 1869 to 1925, brought Shakespeare to the Yiddish language. The playwright Stanislaw Wyspianski put the Polish theater on the cultural map with his carefully crafted presentations. Zbigniew Cybulski was among the many serious actors who appeared on the world's stages and in films. Students from around Poland eagerly flock to Wroclaw to study at the Jerzy Grotowski Actor's Institute and Laboratory Theater and at Henryk Tomaszewski's Mime Theater. As with many Polish cities, Wroclaw also hosts numerous theatrical events. Thousands of fans turn out to see productions staged during Festival of Polish Contemporary Plays.

Polish movies are known for their raw, gritty edge. A hard-won legacy of artistic responsibility and craftsmanship is carried on with young filmmakers like Wladyslaw Pasikowski. His chilling *Dogs 2* described Polish involvement with Russian gangsters. The movie was released in 1993, and quickly became a box-office smash throughout Eastern Europe. Viewers identified with what they saw on the screen. The harsh reality of their daily lives came through on the film.

The Film Center and School in Lodz started the careers of dozens of well-known movie personalities, including Roman Polanski. This famous director came to the United States and made numerous movies. Among them were *Knife in the Water* and *Rosemary's Baby*. On a lighter note, the creator of cartoon animation families the Flintstones and the Jetsons often uses the school's artists for its slapstick animation.

Roman Polanski

Frederic Chopin

Opposite: **Chopin's apartment, around 1830**

Few musicians in the world can equal the skill and dedication of those in Poland. More than one hundred years ago, Frederic Chopin's stirring compositions caused every Pole's heart to swell with pride. His birthplace was in Zelazowa Wola, a village 35 miles (56 km) from Warsaw. Visitors can tour his small house, which is surrounded by a garden exploding with fragrant flowers. Inside the home is a grand piano, where a pianist performs during the summer. Of course, most of the music

Andrzej Wajda

After his father was killed fighting the Nazis during World War II, filmmaker Andrzej Wajda joined the Polish resistance movement. He was only sixteen years old at the time. He attended the Lodz film school and worked for Film Polski, the government-operated film cooperative after he was graduated. This job did not prevent him from tackling serious subjects during the hard, dark days of Communist oppression.

His movies, *Man of Marble* and *Man of Iron*, were known for their fearless liberal viewpoints. In *Ashes and Diamonds*, a young assassin kills a bureaucrat who sold out his country to help the Communists gain power. Wajda's strong beliefs in freedom carried him into other endeavors, as well. Wajda was among the first freely elected members of the new Polish Parliament in 1989.

played was written by the great composer himself. The main Chopin museum is in Warsaw, located in a rebuilt seventeenth-century palace. The building glitters and sparkles with chandeliers and mirrors, much like it was during Chopin's life. Most of the composer's completed music manuscripts are carefully preserved there. In addition, the Museum of Musical Instruments (Muzeum Instrumentow Muzyczynych) in Poznan has several of Chopin's pianos.

Frederic Chopin

Famed pianist Frederic Chopin lived from 1810 to 1849. He began studying music when he was six years old and published his first score when only eight. As an adult, he spent much of his life abroad, living in Paris and on the island of Majorca. Chopin returned briefly to Poland during the revolutionary days of 1830. From this visit, he wrote one piece that his listeners said sounded "like guns hidden in the flowers." After that trip, he never returned to his homeland. Most of his works were very lyrical. Chopin wrote numerous pieces based on Polish dance rhythms. While at the peak of his career, he died of the lung disease called tuberculosis.

Witold Lutoslawski

Arthur Rubinstein (at piano)

Twentieth-century Polish music is just as powerful as that written years earlier. Award-winning Krzystof Penderecki and Witold Lutoslawski are two noted contemporary writers who often drew political themes into their scores, just as Chopin did. In his *Miserere*, Henryk Gorecki paid musical tribute to the brave Solidarity union members who stood up to militia brutality. Performers like Arthur Rubinstein have delighted audiences around the world. His piano concerts were guaranteed to earn him thunderous standing ovations.

Polish music has taken many wonderful turns. Famous performers from Europe and North America flock to an international jazz festival in Warsaw each October. Jazz clubs are popular in all major cities, providing a place for young and old music fans to gather. Everyone seems to be carrying a chunky bass fiddle, a sax, or a trumpet. For fans of singing, an international song festival is held each year in the Baltic seaport of Sopot. It is always a good idea to carry earplugs to the rock concerts that pack in crowds at auditoriums, concert halls, and stadiums. Hard, throbbing music, flashing overhead lights, giant screens, and screaming audiences are all part of the rock scene. Young Poles also have their rave clubs and underground night spots where DJs and live punk bands play.

Quality Work

Polish painters and sculptors are not as internationally known as other cultural contemporaries, but their quality of work is just as high. Jan Matejko, who lived in the mid-1800s, painted canvases that were often more than 20 feet (62 m) long. Many works by modern painters such as Franciszek Starowieyski have been hung in the Center for Contemporary Arts. The gallery opened in 1990 in a seventeenth-century castle. However, Lodz is home to the the Museum of Art (Museum Sztuki). This is the oldest modern art museum in Europe. Painter Wladyslaw Strzeminski, sculptress Katarzyna Kobro, and painter Henryk Stazewski established the museum in 1931. The fact that the artists themselves set up the exhibits gives the gallery a special character.

There are many other museums in Poland. Some are little gems that hold hidden treasures. University graphic students

Artists often sell their paintings on the street.

flock to the Poster Museum (Muzeum Plakatow), located in Warsaw's old Riding School buildings. The designs delight the eye, with their splash of text and hues.

But not all artists show their works in a museum or gallery. The Barbican (City Wall) of Warsaw has traditionally been a place where young artists can showcase their latest imaginative pieces. On pleasant spring and summer days, paintings and weavings hang from the battlements and turrets of the sixteenth-century wall. The fortress architect Giovanni Battista da Vennezia (Jan Baptysta of Venice) would probably be pleased.

Polish Crafts

Polish crafts are also known for their color, texture, and workmanship. Wood, precious stones, paper, straw, crystal, bronze, and silver are among the materials used. Even brightly painted Easter eggs are works of folk art. Anyone who admires craftsmanship immediately turns to the Poles. After World War II, artisans lovingly recreated their country's past glory. They rebuilt castles, markets, public buildings, and homes from the original plans, some of which dated back hundreds of years. They even duplicated the furniture destroyed or stolen during the war.

Just as love of art, music, drama, or theater seems ingrained in Poles, they also appreciate sports and the outdoors. Camping is one of the favorite summertime activities of boys and girls in Poland. They usually set up a tent in a forest clearing and build campfires for heat and cooking. Sometimes, they stay in log huts with modern conveniences like running water and electricity. Swimming or mountain climbing are part of the fun.

Poland is known for its unique handicrafts.

Weddings

Weddings in Poland are similar to the weddings in the United States. Families and friends gather from all over to celebrate. In some villages, a marriage is still an excuse to get all the ethnic costumes out of the closet. The women wear elaborately embroidered dresses and vests over frilly white blouses. The men wear their ballooning trousers tucked into tall black or ox-blood leather boots. Each district of Poland has its special clothing, making it easy to tell the hometown of the wedding couple. It does not make any difference if the bride and groom are poor or wealthy.

There is usually a church ceremony, followed by an extravagant feast. The long tables groan with food. The delicious aroma of beef steak and onions (*rozbratel z cebula*), pickled pigs' knuckles and peas (*nozki wieprzowe z grochem*) and mushroom patties (*kotlety z grzybow*) fill the hall. Vodka, wine, beer, and soft drinks flow. Then the music starts and people dance head-spinning polkas and mazurkas.

Colorful Poland **113**

Downhill skiing is popular in Poland.

That love of exercise and outside fun extends through all the seasons and in urban and rural areas. Downhill and cross-country skiers love Poland's frosty winters. Lively Polish folk songs, sweeping classical music, and even rock 'n' roll warm the crisp air for ice skaters swirling around the rinks. Bicycling along country roads and even table tennis are other popular sports. The village of Leszno has hosted several world championship gliding competitions, with competitors drawn to the soaring mountain breezes. At least ten thousand kids routinely practice weight lifting. Another forty-five thousand play organized basketball. Boxing is also popular. Many kids admire the exploits of Andrew Golota, a champion light-heavyweight who moved to Chicago from Warsaw in the late 1990s. Even though Golota fights far away from Poland, every Pole knows about Chicago. After Warsaw, Chicago has the largest number of Polish people in the world.

Polish athletes always do well competitively. Irena Szewinska-Kirszenstein was nicknamed the Queen of Track for her career. She began running at age fourteen and from eighteen to thirty-four, she had one of the most distinguished careers in international sport. She participated in five Olympic games and won three gold medals.

Poland's Andrew Golota **(left) taking on U.S. boxer Riddick Bowe**

Szewinska-Kirszenstein also broke six world records and was the first woman to hold the records for 100 meters, 200 meters, and 400 meters at the same time. In the 1990s, Szewinska-Kirszenstein was a member of the International Amateur Athletic Federation women's committee.

There are other Polish speedsters, as well. Gleaming trophies line the walls of Sobieslaw Zasada's home in Kraków. Zasada always seems to be in a hurry. After all, he won numerous auto racing championships, including the grueling Grand Prix in Argentina and other international competitions.

Renata Mauer won the first gold medal of the 1996 Summer Olympic Games.

Polish athletes won seven gold medals, five silver, and five bronze medals at the 1996 Summer Olympics in Atlanta, Georgia. This ranking placed them fifteenth among all the competing nations. Renata Mauer of Poland even won the very first gold awarded at the games, for her victory in the air-rifle competition. Poland's president, Aleksander Kwasniewski, was in the audience to cheer Wlodzimierz Zawadzki, who won his gold in Greco-Roman wrestling.

Soccer

Polish kids love soccer. An estimated 300,000 young people play some level of the national sport. Only the top players from the country's clubs can join the national team to play in the World Cup, the world's most popular sporting event. The Cup finals are held every four years, in which sixteen of the world's best national teams compete. In the 1974 games held in Germany, the Polish team placed third in the world. The players, coached by Kazimierz Gorski, defeated the much-favored, fast-moving Brazilians in the consolation match.

Millions of television viewers watched the battle as Poland's Robert Gadocha and Kazimierz Deyna outperformed the speedy South Americans. Grzegorz Lato scored the winning goal that won the match, 1–0. The Polish team also qualified for the 1978 World Cup games in Argentina, but were defeated in the early rounds of play. Regardless, the players were still considered heroes at home.

Almost every Pole loves fishing. Top-notch fishing can be found in the Mazurian Lake district of northeastern Poland: Mamry (Mamree), Dargin (Darkin) and Szelak Wielki (Shelok Vyelky). In some mountain streams, a delicious carp-like fish called the *glowacia* can be lured into a skillful fishing fan's frying pan. It would have to a big pan because some glowacie weigh 40 pounds (18 kg) or more. The best months for fishing are August, September, and October.

With all this culture and sport, it's a wonder that the Poles aren't exhausted.

Many Poles enjoy the sport of fishing.

Jan's Day

It is barely sunup. Jan stretches out from under the bedcovers. It is time to get up and look after the family cows. The sun is just peeking over the crags rearing high above the family farm. The rays touch the larch and birch trees carpeting the steep slopes behind Jan's large home. The century-old house is made of thick, heavy logs peeled of their bark and washed so much they appear a dull yellow. Soon the chill autumn air will warm in the dawn's sunshine bath.

B<small>UT NOW</small>, J<small>AN WOULD RATHER</small> snuggle under the heavy quilt stuffed with its fluffy, soft, goose down. But his nose is tickled by the sweet scent of breakfast being fixed by his mother. She is the world's best breakfast maker. Everyone will soon be going to mass in the village church, which is a brisk walk 2 miles (3.2 km) away. The family car is saved for longer trips to the city and for bad weather.

From his bed in the house loft, he hears the footsteps of his older brother. Juliusz is home visiting from Warsaw University. Although only in his second year, Juliusz already wants to be like Professor Jan Michalowski, a famous Polish archaeologist who uncovered the exotic temples of Faras in Egypt. Juliusz hopes to travel on a study tour there next summer so he keeps Jan up-to-date with his plans.

Warsaw University

Helena Modjeska

The boys' sisters, Helena and Jadwiga (whose nickname is Jaga), have been awake for a long time and are already helping their mother with the meal. Jaga was named after one of the queens of Poland and Helena was named after Helena Modjeska, a famous Polish actress who toured all over the world in the late 1800s and settled in San Francisco. Their mom, who did some acting in school, thought of the name. Their dad is already outside, splitting more dry logs for the fire. With Juliusz away at school, there are always extra chores for everyone in the family. However, all the neighbors share in heavier work of the harvest, so there are plenty of helping hands when necessary.

Jan's family lives in the Sudeten Mountains of southern Poland. The ridges and cliffs surrounding their valley home are not as lofty as some of Poland's other mountain ranges. But to Jan, they are high enough. He loves hiking through the deep forests beyond the wheat fields. One of his hobbies is hunting for mushrooms. For now, Jan has to rush outside to feed and milk the cows. Even though it is Sunday, the hungry animals don't like to wait.

On crisp days like this, Jan loves coming back inside to the heat and wonderful smells. In the countryside, the food is prepared on wood stoves. From the farmhouses throughout Jan's mountain valley, chimney smoke wafts upward as other families prepare breakfast. Jan's mom boils water for tea. The hottest temperature is in the center of the massive ceramic stove. A teapot steams away. Elaborate hand-painted tiles line the outside of the stove. The tiles radiate heat, with the flat surfaces on top being warm enough to use for baking. Jan's uncle, aunt, and cousins live in Warsaw. They have a modern gas stove. Whenever Jan goes to visit them, he doesn't think their kitchen seems quite as warm and cozy as his does.

A modern apartment building in Wroclaw

Breakfast Treat

Breakfast for mountain families is always a feast, especially on Sundays. Jan's dad and mom, like all their neighbors, work hard caring for their animals and crops. They need a good meal in the morning to get started. Today, there is homemade sausage made of a mixture of veal and pork. The family's own calves and pigs were butchered to make the sausage. Jan loves the dark peasant bread made by Helena, who is getting to be almost as good a baker as their mom. Jan cuts the bread into huge chunks, which will be eaten with pungent, smelly goat cheese. Sometimes, he eats a drier cheese made from cow's milk. Both are delicious.

The kids love putting honey on their bread. Their dad collects the honey from several hives at the far end of one of their pastures. Bees gather nectar from the mountain blossoms

Babka and tea

attracted by the sticky sweet scent of the flowers. Usually, plenty of desserts round out breakfast. Jan and Juliusz always argue who gets the last piece of a pound cake called babka. To make peace, their mother promises to send another babka with Juliusz when he leaves for the university on Monday.

At breakfast, Juliusz tells Jan and their sisters about university life in Warsaw. After classes, he and his friends hang out at a milk bar (*bar mleczny*) near school. Like students everywhere, they are always hungry and can get inexpensive snacks at a milk bar. A bar in Poland is not a place to drink alcohol, but a small restaurant that serves inexpensive food. Juliusz and his pals stand up and eat at high tables or a countertop in the window facing the street.

Sometimes, his crowd goes to cafés (*kawiarni*) for special occasions. Tea and coffee are served in tall glasses instead of cups. It is necessary to hold the glasses at their very top, so fingers don't get burned. *Kompot*, a fruit drink, is also popular. But those places are usually expensive on a student's income. Although the university is free, as are all schools in Poland, Juliusz works in a bookstore to earn spending money.

Their father, who just came into the kitchen, chimes in. When he was younger, he had been elected head of a farmers' cooperative during Poland's Communist regime. Years ago, all the farm leaders were called to Kraków for a convention. Some of them, including Jan's father, were treated for dinner at the Wierzynek. This is Poland's oldest restaurant, opened in the 1300s. It still serves meals fit for the crowned heads of Europe, according to Jan's dad. Casimir the Great and German Emperor Charles IV had supper here, he said. King

The Wierzynek

Food

When it comes to food, Poland is lucky to be a cross-roads country. Because the Polish court had so many alliances with other European nobles, they also shared the talents of their chefs as well as those of their musicians, artists, and writers. Czech, French, Hungarian, Russian, and German influences received a special local touch. Consider that the Polish word for fresh, green vegetables is wloszczyzna, which means things Italian. Even invaders from the Far East left the Poles a taste for pungent spices, thick tea, and flavorful artichokes.

The noon meal is usually considered dinner, starting with smoked fish (ryby wedzone) or smoked ham (szynka). Soup (zupa) is served as the first course. The most popular soup, barszcz, is made with a tantalizing mix of beets, carrots, and beef. A big plop

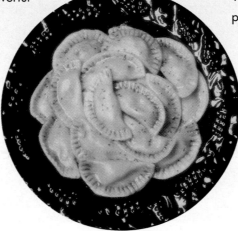

of sour cream is usually added on top. Several small stuffed pies are placed on the table as an accompaniment. Filled with meat, they are called paszteciki. Other favorite soups are cabbage (kapusniak), potatoes (kartoflanka), or mushrooms (grzybowa). If anyone is still hungry, there are dumplings (pierogi) filled with meat, cheese or vegetables, as well as roast pork (pieczony schab) or fish. If children are lucky, there might be some ice cream (lody) or crepes (nalesniki) for dessert.

A country dinner consists of sausage, pierogi, fresh bread, and berry jam. One dish is made from potatoes and sour milk, which tastes like yogurt. Sunday lunch is often chicken and dumplings and potatoes. Sheep's milk cheese is hand-molded into an egg shape. This smoky cheese has a distinct flavor, one not easily forgotten.

Inside the Wierzynek, Poland's oldest restaurant, dating back to the 1300s.

Louis I of Hungary especially liked the poppy seed cake for dessert, after a stomach-stretching meal of wild boar and truffles. Jan's dad didn't have the wild boar, since they didn't serve that anymore, but he did have similar cakes for dessert. Of course, that all-expense paid trip was well before his dad became a leader in Rural Solidarity, a farmers' union that helped get rid of the Communist system in Poland. His dad still laughs about the good trip he got out of the old government.

After hearing all these stories about food, Jan is getting full. But he thinks, "Maybe I'll become a chef. At least I won't have to milk the cows anymore." There are many famous restaurants where Jan could work if he gave up farm life. Diners could be served his stuffed eel at the Kaszubska in Gdansk, roast duck at the Kamienne Schodki in Warsaw, or chicken shish kebab at the Obrochtowka in Zakopane.

After chores and breakfast, Jan and his family clean up and leave for church. They wear their best suits and dresses even though they walk along a dusty mountain road. There they meet and talk with friends also on their way to church. Some of the older people in the parish regularly wear their traditional local costumes for Sunday services. The men have feathers in their red-and-black hats and the women's dresses and vests are adorned with lovely long ribbons. Jan's mom and

Easter Sunday

sisters also have such fancy clothes, which are saved for weddings and holidays. Easter is one of Jan's favorite holidays because he helps paint intricate colors on the eggs. He also likes the day after Easter, which is called Wet Monday. On this day, the children run around dumping water on each other. Older boys chase their girlfriends and sprinkle perfume on them.

But it is a long time until Easter. So Jan is looking forward to All Soul's Day (November 2), which is the next big Polish holiday. On the evening before, the family visits the church cemetery where their deceased relatives are buried. From the front steps of the church, Jan can see the headstone on the graves of his mother's parents. His grandparents met while resistance fighters battling the Nazis during World War II. His grandmother walked with a limp because she had been wounded. She was only seventeen at the time and his grandfather was nineteen when they were married in a secret hideout.

Bialy

The famed *bialy*, a doughy roll akin to the bagel, originated in Bialystok. This city, noted for its linen and leather industries, is a two-hour drive from Warsaw. Many Jewish families from here emigrated to the United States around the turn of the century. They brought recipes for their native foods with them, including that of the bialy. With cream cheese, the bialy is a wonderful taste treat. Close to Bialystok is the Bialowieza National Park, home of the Polish bison.

Polish families visit cemeteries to honor their deceased relatives.

They didn't talk much about those terrible days except to say they were proud to defend their country. Jan hopes that he would be that brave if he needed to be. Jan never saw his other grandparents. They died during the war when the Nazis burned their village. Jan reads about Polish heroes and heroines at school. He thinks their exploits were exciting, but they occurred long ago. But his grandparents were closer. That's why visiting the cemetery is always special.

Play Ball

Polish girls enjoying a spring festival

After church, Jan and his friends kick around a soccer ball in the playground as the grown-ups talk. The boys dream of playing ball in the stadium in Chorzow, a city that is only a few hours' train trip from home. The stadium holds 100,000 people. Jan dreams of making the winning goal in a championship game there. He is already a good wing, one of the forward players and a leading scorer, on his school team. His coach urges him to continue practicing so that someday he will be as good as Adam Musial, who played on Poland's World Cup team.

After church, it is already early afternoon. Everyone goes home. Jan has to write a report for his science class. He has three more years left before he can attend secondary school, which is like high school in North America. He wants to work hard like Juliusz and pass his examinations so he can attend a college. Jan has a big selection from which to choose because Poland has ten universities. He is already thinking of going to Jagiellonian University, the country's oldest university. The school was founded in 1364 in Kraków. Jan thinks he would like it there because he loves history. Since he is also a good reader and enjoys math, his parents encourage him to do his best.

Or there is always agricultural school, Jan thinks. He could come back to the farm and help his dad. That way he could always keep up with his mushroom hunting. There is plenty of time to decide. Now his task is to finish his homework, attend to the livestock again, and lay out his clothes for school tomorrow. His parents will take Juliusz to the train station for his long ride back to Warsaw. Just before he falls asleep that night, Jan smells that babka being baked. He hopes his mom baked an extra one for him.

A primary school in Poland

Timeline

Polish History

Poland and Lithuania unite.	**1569**
End of the Jagiellonion Dynasty and beginning of elected monarchy	**1572**
Sweden invades Poland	**1655**
The Seym, the Polish Parliament, adopt a Constitution, the second of its kind in the world. It is modeled on the U.S Constitution. (May 3)	**1791**
The new Polish Constitution is crushed by the partition of Poland by Russia, Prussia and Austria.	**1793 – 1795**
Foundation of the first Polish revolutionary workers party, Proletariat	**1882**
Poland declared an independent republic (November 11)	**1918**
Poland is crushed in a lightning quick attack by Nazi Germany and Russia, who then partition the country into two parts.	**1939**
The systematic murder of Jews begins in the concentration camps of Poland, killing almost 4 million people by 1944.	**1941 – 1944**
Poland is liberated from Nazi Germany and comes under indirect rule by the Soviet Union (July)	**1944**
The Soviet sponsored Polish Committee of National Liberation takes over government. (January 1)	**1945**
Creation of Solidarity, a trade union organization, and led by Lech Walesa (July)	**1980**
Walesa given Nobel Peace Prize (October)	**1983**
The end of almost 45 years of Communist domination comes with a coalition government consisting of Solidarity, The United Peasants Party, and the Democratic Party. (August 24)	**1989**
Membership in Warsaw Pact ends.	**1991**
Final withdrawal of Soviet troops is complete.	**1994**
Lech Walesa loses presidency to Aleksander Kwasniewski, a former communist party member (November 5)	**1995**

World History

1776	The Declaration of Independence is signed.
1789	The French Revolution begins.
1865	The American Civil War ends.
1914	World War I breaks out.
1917	The Bolshevik Revolution brings Communism to Russia.
1929	Worldwide economic depression begins.
1939	World War II begins, following the German invasion of Poland.
1957	The Vietnam War starts.
1989	The Berlin Wall is torn down, as Communism crumbles in Eastern Europe.
1996	Bill Clinton re-elected U.S. president.

Fast Facts

Official name: Republic of Poland

Capital: Warsaw

Official language:	Polish
Official religion:	None
National anthem:	"Jeszcze Polska nie Zginela" ("Poland Has Not Yet Perished While We Are Still Alive"; sometimes called "Dabrowski Mazurka"
Government:	Multiparty republic with two legislative houses
Area:	120,728 square miles (312,684 sq km)
Bordering countries:	Poland is situated in Eastern Europe. To the north lies the Baltic Sea; to the northeast, Lithuania; to the east, Belarus; to the southeast, Ukraine; to the west, Germany; and to the south, Czech Republic and Slovakia.
Highest elevation:	Rysy Peak at 8,196 feet (2,499 m)
Lowest elevation:	The Vistula Delta at 6 feet (1.8 m)
Average temperatures:	*Winter:* 23° to 30° F (−5°C to 0°C) *Summer:* 60° to 70° F (16° to 21° C)
Average annual rainfall:	24 inches (610 mm)
National population: (1995 est.)	38,504,700

Population of largest cities in Poland: (1995 est.)

Warsaw	2,316,000
Lodz	842,300
Kraków	751,500
Wroclaw	642,900
Poznan	589,300
Gdansk	466,700

Famous Landmarks: Royal Castle (Zamek Krolewski) in Warsaw
Cathedral of St. John (Bazylika Swietego Jana)
   in Warsaw
St. Florain's Gate (Brama Florianska) in Kraków
Auschwitz (Oswiecim) 30 miles (48 km) west
   of Kraków
Solidarity Monument in Gdansk
Dtugi Targ Square in Gdansk
Town Hall (Ratusz) in Poznan
Nozyks Synagogue (the only synagogue to survive
   World War II) in Warsaw

Industry: Nearly 42 percent of the Gross Domestic Product
(GDP) of Poland comes from industry, with manufacturing at 23.2%, agriculture at 7.1%, and
mining at 4.8%.

Currency: One zloty equals 100 groszy. The 1997 rate
exchange: U.S. 1$ = 3.16 new zlotys

Weights and measures: Metric system

Literacy: 98.7%

Common Polish words and phrases:

Good morning!	*Dzien dobry* (dzhehn do-bri)
How are you?	*Jak sie masz* (Yahk syeh mahsh)
Do you speak English?	*Czy pan mowi po angielsku* (Chi pahn movee po ahngyehlskoo)
I understand.	*Rozumiem* (razoomyehn)
My name is…	*Nazywam sie…* (nahzivahm syeh…)
I'm hungry.	*Jestem glodny* (Yehstehm gwodni)
I'd like dessert, please.	*Prosze o deser* (Prosheh o dehsehr)
Glad to know you.	*Milo mi* (Meewo mee)
Thank you	*Dziekuje* (Dzhhehnkooyeh)
Good-Bye	*Do widzenia* (Do veedzehnah)

To Find Out More

Nonfiction

▶ Adler, David A. *Child of the Warsaw Ghetto*. New York: Holiday House, 1995.

▶ Budrewicz, O. *Introduction to Poland*. Miami: The American Institute of Polish Culture, 1985.

▶ Davies, Norman. *Heart of Europe: A Short History of Poland*. Oxford: Clarendon Press, 1984.

▶ Dobbs, Michael, Karol, K.S., and Dessa Travisan. *Poland: Solidarity: Walesa*. New York: McGraw-Hill, 1981.

▶ Gronowicz, Antoni. *Polish Profiles: The Land, the People and Their History*. Westport, CT: L. Hill, 1976.

▶ Moscinski, A. *Tracing Our Polish Roots*. Santa Fe: John Muir Publications, 1994.

▶ Pula, James S. and M. B. Biskupski. *Heart of the Nation: Polish Literature and Culture*. New York: Columbia University Press, 1993.

▶ Roberts, Kenneth. *Poland's First Post-Communist Generation*. Brookfield, VT: Ashgate Publishing Company, 1995.

▶ Stephenson, Jill and Alfred Bloch. *Poland*. New York: Hippocrene Books, 1991.

▶ Weclawowicz, Gregorz. *Contemporary Poland*. Boulder, CO: Westview Press, 1996.

Fiction

▶ Goscilo, Helena. *Russian and Polish Women's Fiction*. Knoxville: University of Tennessee Press, 1985.

▶ Morska, Irena. *Polish Authors of Today and Yesterday*. New York: S.F. Vanni Press, 1947.

Videotapes

▶ *Poland: 1000 years of History and Culture*, Parts 1–4. Produced and directed by Roger Conant, 1989.

Websites

▶ **Poland Home Page**
http://info.fuw.edu.pl/pl/PolandHome.html
This collection of Poland-related websites gives information ranging from the time of the next flight to Warsaw to quotes from the Polish stock exchange.

▶ **The Tatra Mountains Virtual Tourist**
http://www.cs.put.poznan.pl/holidays/tatry/
A virtual tour of the spectacular Tatra mountains.

▶ **Centre for Contemporary Art, Warsaw**
http://www.sunsite.icm.edu.pl/culture/csw/
An attractive and informative cybertour of this museum housed in a seventeenth-century castle.

Warsaw
http://www.icm.edu.pl/warsaw/
This city page is an tribute to both Old and New Warsaw. This site is filled with history and pictures.

Central Europe.com
http://www.centraleurope.com/
Provides a wide range of information about the government, constitution, politics, transportation, the environment, and the people.

Polish Embassy in London
http://www.poland-embassy.org.uk/
The Polish Embassy Web page contains information about Poland, its political institutions, culture, economy, and many useful links to interesting sites in Poland.

Organizations and Embassies

Polish Cultural Institute
34 Portland Place
London W1N 4HQ
(011) 0171-636-6032
Fax: (011) 0171-637-2190
pci-1ond@pcidir.demon.co.uk

Index

Meet the Author

MARTIN HINTZ had made several trips to Poland during his writing career. His first visit was in 1974 as a newspaper reporter covering the thirtieth anniversary celebrations marking the liberation of Warsaw at the end of World War II. He also was on hand during the heyday of the Solidarity Trade Union movement and watched as Poles reveled in the fresh air of their new freedom. His touring took him to many of the major cities of Poland, as well as throughout the countryside.

He even collected a jaywalking ticket on one trip! It was after midnight when he walked across an intersection on one of Warsaw's major downtown streets. He was on his way to the Associated Press office to file a story. Two policemen waved him over and presented him with the ticket. Apparently, Hintz should have used a pedestrian tunnel to get to the other side of the road.

On his trips, he visited the site of the Warsaw ghetto, learned to drink hot tea from a glass, danced in the night clubs, attended a wedding, and meet dozens of wonderful, friendly people.

For Poland, Hintz used this firsthand background to set the stage for the rest of the book. He updated this early material with library research, searching the Internet, and interviews with Poles and Polish Americans.

Hintz lives in Milwaukee, Wisconsin, one of North America's most Polish cities. For generations, Polish immigrants and their descendants worked in the community's factories, breweries, and other industries. They are among the city's leading citizens, with judges, politicians, clergy, and educators among their ranks. Each summer, Milwaukee hosts a major Polish Fest on the city's lakefront festival grounds. That keeps Hintz in touch with all the great food, music, and dancing of Poland.

And Milwaukee is only 90 miles (145 km) north of Chicago, considered the world's second largest "Polish" city after Warsaw. On jaunts to the Windy City, there is always great barszcz to find and sup. Chicago's many Polish neighborhood restaurants serve this great beef and vegetable soup. Hintz is always on the quest for the best.

Photo Credits

Photographs ©:

Archive Photos: 101 top (The Jewish Museum), 24 top left, 105 top;
Art Resource: 108 bottom (Giraudon), 48, 109 bottom (Erich Lessing);
Corbis-Bettmann: 42, 47, 49, 50 top left, 50 bottom, 51 bottom, 55 top, 91 bottom left, 110 bottom, 120;
Envision: 123 bottom (Peter Johansky), 122 (Rudy Miller);
Gamma-Liason: 108 top (Benainous-Duclos), 22 (Georges De Keerle), 106 right (Laski Diffusion), 113 bottom (Boleslaw Edelhajt), 27 (Dave Nagel), 72 top (Malecki Piotr), 81 bottom (James Schnepf), 91 bottom right (Stachowicz), 109 top (Krzysztof Wojick), 106 left;
H. Armstrong Roberts: 83 top (Arthur Mauritius), 99 (R. Richardson), 24 top right, 90, 112 (A. Tovy), 126 top (Zefa-U.K.), 10;
Herb Swanson: 72 bottom;
The Image Works: 91 top (John Eastcott/YVA Momatiuk);
Imapress/Archive Photos: 75, 76;
Imperial War Museum/Archive Photos: 52;
James Marshall: 32 top, 33, 66, 68 botom, 81 top, 95, 123 top;
National Geographic Image Collection: 32 bottom, 37 top (Raymond K. Gehman), 43 (Zbigniew Jans Lutyk), 39, 57, 74, 96 bottom, 98 bottom, 110 top (James L. Stanfield);
New York Public Library, Research Division: 46 bottom;
New York Times/Archive Photos: 107;
The Niels Bohr Library: 50 top right (Harlingue);
North Wind Picture Archives: 88 top, 89, 97 top;
Omni-Photo Communications: 103 bottom, 113 top (Amos Zezmer);
Panos Pictures: 17, 70, 87, 101 bottom (David Constantine), 73 (Jeremy Hartley), 29, 40, 84 (Liba Taylor), spine, 24 bottom, 25 left, 78, 119 (Gregory Wrona);
Photo Researchers: 9, 58, 80 (Boutin/Explorer), 67 bottom (Brossard/Explorer), 98 top, 125, 88 bottom (Eastcott/Momatiuk), 36 (John Eastcott/YVA Momatiuk), 77 (Guillou/Explorer), 126 bottom (Philippon/Explorer), 35 bottom (Leonard Lee Rue III), 35 top (St. Meyers/OKAPIA), 31 (Mary M. Thacher);
Polish National Tourist Office: 124, 133 (Michal Grychowski), 7 top, 16, 20, 21, 37 bottom, 92, 93, 114, 117, 132;
Polish National Tourist Office in Chicago: 2;
Reuters/Archive Photos: 64 (David Brauchli), 55 bottom (Joseph Czarnecki), 116 (Nick Didlick), 65 top (Damazy Kwaitkowski), 65 bottom (Kevin Lamarque), 115 (Ray Stubblebine);
Sovfoto/Eastfoto: 53 (Ken Hotz), 30, 46 top, 105 bottom;
Tom Stack & Associates: 19, 25 right, 28, 34, 79, 83 bottom, 94, 97 bottom, 118, 121, 130 (Witold Skrypszak);
Tony Stone Images: 86 (Glen Allison), 103 top right (Geoff Johnson), 104 (Chris Neidenthal), 38 (Zygaunt Nowak Solins), 67 top (Andy Sotirou), 23 (Steven Weinberg), 68 top, 69;
UPI/Corbis-Bettmann: 51 top, 54, 96 top, 103 top left;
Visual Contact: 8 (Marek Baczkowski), 15 (T. Freda), cover, back cover, 7 bottom, 12, 13, 61, 127, 131 (Robert Szykowski).